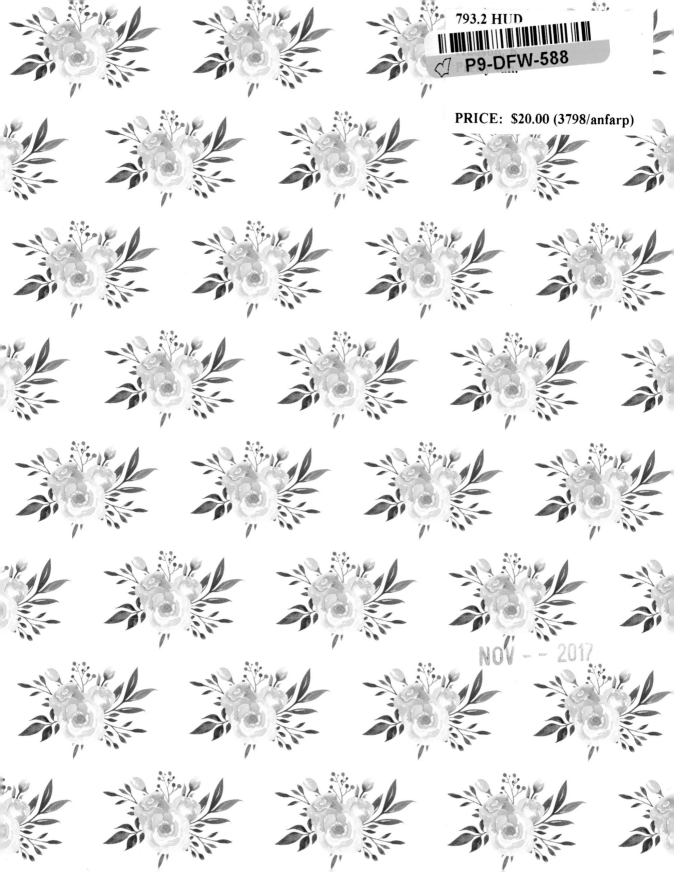

PRETTY FUN

CREATING AND CELEBRATING
A LIFETIME OF TRADITION

KATE HUDSON

with

RACHEL HOLTZMAN

PHOTOGRAPHS BY AMY NEUNSINGER

DEY ST.
An Imprint of WILLIAM MORROW

FIRST DEY STREET HARDCOVER PUBLISHED
FIRST EDITION

Library of Congress Cataloging-in-Publication Data
has been applied for.

Illustrations: Shutterstock.com
Photographs on pages 44-45, 124, 138-139, 182-183, 214-215, 226:
Shutterstock.com
Photographs on pages 4, 7, 25, 54, 102, 103, 134, 178, 208:
courtesy of the author.

ISBN 978-0-06-268576-6 (hardcover)
978-0-06-283557-4 (B&N Black Friday signed edition)
978-0-06-283558-1 (BAM signed edition)
978-0-06-283685-4 (Target edition)

17 18 19 20 21   LSC   10 9 8 7 6 5 4 3 2 1

For my Mom and Pa
because creating these traditions
all started with you.

Love you to the moon and back.

CONTENTS

PART TWO

Pretty Excited!

What lies at the heart of this book, and what makes this project such a special one to me, are the lessons I learned from a very early age about the importance of gathering, marking events big and small, and enjoying the company of the people who matter to you most.

A NEW WAY TO GATHER

THIS MIGHT COME as a surprise, but this is not a book about parties. Don't worry, we'll talk about decorations and delicious food and all the really fun, creative ways to celebrate a special occasion—and we're going to have a *great* time doing it—but that's not what's at the heart of this book. What makes this project such a special one to me, are the lessons I learned from a very early age about the importance of gathering, marking events big and small, and enjoying the company of the people who matter to you most.

Growing up, my parents had careers that demanded a lot of them—a lot of travel, busy schedules, and a lot of responsibilities that took our entire family outside of the home. Despite those demanding schedules, they were always present for us kids, and they let us know that our time together was meaningful by making the most of it, which in our house meant lots of food, drink, conversation, and laughter. For our big, crazy, blended family, they made it a priority to preserve what you might consider traditional values in a very nontraditional life.

In our childhood home everyone was welcome. If we were home, the door was open. There'd be snacks in the fridge and music on the stereo. You could put your feet on the furniture, and nobody minded if you stayed for dinner because there'd usually be a big pot of something on the stove (my mom is the one-pot queen!), like elk stew or chicken and dumplings, making the house smell so wonderful and cozy. On those days, there wasn't any question about what all of our friends would be doing after school, because they'd always end up at our house, sharing the day's stories with my parents, unwinding, and feeling right at home.

If it was a Sunday night, we'd have a simple, laid-back dinner, and you can bet that by the time the meal was ready there'd be fifteen, twenty people at the table. It wasn't because my mom was an amazing cook (though she most definitely is—and her beef stroganoff recipe is on page 96 to prove it!); it was because our house was a place where people could *connect*. It was a house full of the vibrant sounds of people, and it filled us all with so much joy. There was never anything forced or overly planned about it; it was just a way of life.

Sure, my parents loved to entertain—every year they hosted a Christmas party, complete with a carol sing-along with official lyric books, and Thanksgiving was essentially a big game of musical chairs, because they never said no to anyone joining us, whether it was family, friends, friends of friends, or folks with nowhere else to go—but it was the everyday gatherings that made our house special.

Well, that kind of thing rubs off on you. So when I started my own household in my twenties, I carried these traditions with me—and gave them my unique twist. I wanted to create that kind of environment for my kids and for my own tribe of friends and adopted family, where everyone felt like they could kick off their shoes, sit on anything, and knew that if they spilled their wine or even had a glass too many, they'd still be invited back. I wanted people to feel safe in my home and, of course, have a great time! My philosophy toward hosting is "*Pretty Fun*"—nothing too perfect, nothing too fussy, just the right amount of attention to detail to look great, but not so stuffy you can't enjoy yourself.

It's a philosophy that's deeply connected to the concepts I explored in my first book, *Pretty Happy*. Writing that was its own kind of celebration—of finally discovering how to slow down, tune in, and figure out how to give myself what I need to feel my absolute best, inside and out. It was the culmination of a lot of soul-searching, where I finally realized how important true connection was and how to take care of myself in a more complete way: Mind *and* body. Body *and* soul. Pilates *and* hot yoga *and* spinning *and* sometimes just a nice long hike. It's what I'd call holistic and balanced. Once I realized that nourishing every little piece of myself in a forgiving, loving way made me *Pretty Happy*, I had to share it! And this book is a natural extension of that. Because here's the thing: gathering is just as crucial a part of self-care as eating well and having a movement practice. Plus the very same lessons I learned about taking better care of myself make for even more meaningful gathering. It all adds up to one big, beautiful cycle that can infuse your life with that much more pleasure, significance, rootedness, and contentment. If that doesn't sound like it's worth its own little party, then I don't know what does!

AYURVEDIC MEDICINE (an ancient Indian prescription for health that integrates mind, body, and spirit) teaches that true wellness is achieved only when you treat the *whole* person. It's a powerful idea that I've incorporated into my life, and I'm a firm believer that even if I'm honoring my body with the most healthful foods and exercise and being super-disciplined with meditation or breath work, I won't truly feel grounded or even-keeled unless I'm also taking care of my spirit. I know that might sound a little New Agey, but seriously, think about how you feel when you laugh. Like *really* laugh. Or how happy you are when surrounded by your closest friends, feeling seen, heard, and supported. Or when you're sharing stories about your day with your family over a meal that you prepared yourself. Doesn't sound so "out there" now, does it? Those are all spirit-feeding, soul-satisfying things that would make anyone feel good. And that's exactly what gathering—and *Pretty Fun*—is all about. I don't have an open-door policy at my house because I'm a huge party animal, and I don't put in the extra effort to deck out my living room/garden/pool with theme-coordinated decorations and yummy, healthful snacks because I want to show off. It's because connecting with the people I care about

makes me feel complete. Taking care of them and creating a space to have a good time is how I feel nourished. When you summon that intention in yourself (something we'll be talking about quite a bit in this book), even the simplest, most spur-of-the-moment get-together can feel substantive and important.

One reason getting together is so powerful is because it keeps us connected with our tribe. Our network of trusted loved ones—whether it's friends, siblings, parents, grandparents, aunts and uncles, children, gurus, mentors, or partners (past and present)—is our support system, our safety net. They're the people who you know will be there to share the good and lift you up after the bad and the ugly. Bonding with your tribe, even if it's a collection of strays that you've picked up over the years, gives you an increased sense of security, confidence, and peace. And when we get together, we get to honor that—and usually have a *Pretty Fantastic* time!

Gathering is also something that allows us to express gratitude—a key ingredient for staying in touch with what matters most in life. It's been proven that people who make a practice of being thankful experience more joy. That makes sense, because when you say a little thanks, you're putting yourself in a sunnier, more positive space, which makes it easier to see the great and let go of the not-so-great. It's why I take a few minutes every day to acknowledge a couple of things I'm grateful for, even if it's just a beautiful flower blooming outside my window or making tacos with my kids. On one level, when we invite people to our home and make them feel special, we're expressing our gratitude for them. On another level, you can use gratitude as a *reason* to gather, like a Mother's Day brunch or an It's Finally Sunny! impromptu party. No matter what, you can always make space for gratitude at a gathering, whether it's going around the room and asking people what they loved most about their summer or having everyone share a kind thought about the guest of honor. Throughout this book, I'll share ideas for how you can tuck these simple but powerful moments into your own gatherings.

Over the years, I've developed what I like to think of as a celebration "practice"—and I do mean practice, because I've done a lot of it. I *love* a party! From Halloween blowouts and over-the-top themed birthday parties (which you might have seen on social media) to football Sundays to spur-of-the-moment girls' nights, there's no reason good enough not to get together in my book. Even my friends will ask if they can have a party at my house, and the answer is always "Yes!"— because it makes me feel really good to help, and if the only thing standing between someone and their dream party is the right space, far be it from me to stop them!

What I've learned through this celebration practice is that a little mindfulness goes a long way. Just as mindfulness in meditation can help us focus on the present moment and make sense of our thoughts and feelings, taking a moment to do a little internal inventory before planning a gathering can be just as meaningful. It doesn't matter whether I'm doing a done-up, schmancy affair like New Year's Eve or a super-casual, last-minute backyard bocce tournament, I'm always thinking about how I can get people (and myself!) to breathe a little easier, laugh a little louder, and just let go whenever possible. The secret I've discovered is that it all comes back to *intention*.

You've probably set an intention before—maybe it was for a yoga class or when starting to work on a new life goal like losing weight, saving money, or getting a new job. Intention is a powerful thing because it roots us to our motivation, to our *why*. For me, a significant example is when I built my athletic clothing company, Fabletics. I didn't want it to be just about going to the gym or looking a certain way. I wanted people to feel the same inspiration that I do when it comes to working out. So I reconnected with my own *why*, the reason that keeps me motivated to push my body to new limits or at the very least to push through the noise of what I "should" look like. It's because exercise helps me plug in to the strength and resilience that fortifies me in every other area of my life—and that's exactly what I wanted other women (and men) to be able to experience too.

When you dig a little deeper, when you connect with your *why*, then suddenly whatever you're doing takes on a lot more meaning. The same thing goes for a party. As we'll talk about much more throughout this book, setting an intention for a celebration is what turns a *party* into a *gathering*.

It's tuning in to why you're getting together and then creating a space that supports that, from the theme to the menu to the decorations to the favors. Those details—no matter how inexpensive or lavish—are what set the mood, and that mood is what makes guests feel like family (unless they already are, in which case, like royalty!).

In the following chapters, I'll be sharing some of my favorite ways to celebrate with mindfulness and intention, from the sweet (Mom's Favorite Things Brunch) to the spontaneous (a pop-up pajama party with all your best girlfriends), the quintessential (Thanksgiving with All the Pies) to the meaningful (a family night dinner on a quiet Saturday). We'll talk about crucial details—the bar! the food! the lighting! the playlist!—and also how to chuck it all when it's time to not sweat the small stuff. I'll help you arrange a cheese board to end all cheese boards, whip up on-the-fly dinners, and make the perfect thank-you toast. In the end, it's about helping you find your unique entertaining style and getting friends and family together.

As you may have noticed, though, this book isn't like other traditional "entertaining" guides. You won't find set menus here or step-by-step instructions for flower arrangements. I'm not going to present you with a blueprint for how exactly to throw a party, down to the placement of your silverware. That's not because I don't know how to or because I don't completely love those things (because I do and I do!); it's because I don't want to step on your unique spirit and experience. Learning how to throw a great party comes from *doing,* not reading about it in a book. And a gathering will feel much more genuine if it's coming from you, not from what I tell you to do. That said, I'll be here to guide you through the basics, sprinkle on some inspiration, stir in a dollop of my time-tested wisdom, and most important, get you started with your own celebration practice and help you connect with your intention. I've included party concepts from some of my favorite occasions to celebrate (a mix of my family's time-honored traditions, personalized and updated seasonal classics, and jazzed-up rotational staples, like a bachelorette party, back-to-school party, and all-grown-up birthday party) and tossed in some of my go-to recipes, including many that are big on flavor, yet skip ingredients that will keep you from feeling like your light, bright self. We'll talk about how to find your own unique entertaining aesthetic and how to stock your fridge and pantry so a tasty spread is never more than a few minutes away. From there, it's up to you to tune it in, turn it up, and have a *Pretty Fun* time.

PART ONE

PRETTY PREPARED

CHAPTER ONE

STARTING YOUR CELEBRATION PRACTICE

SURE, THERE ARE the obvious reasons why it's usually a great idea to throw a party: to have a good time, to make someone feel special, to mark an occasion, to eat great food, to dress up, to dance, to not spend too much time alone, and so on. But there's something deeper happening when we *gather*. Taking the time to get together with people we love and creating a space that feels out of the ordinary isn't just about snacks and margaritas. It connects us with something humans have been doing pretty much since the beginning of time, when we were hanging out together in caves and huts.

Back in those days, people realized how important it was to align themselves with a tribe. Sure, the pickings were slimmer—it was usually anyone who was around and/or related—but the wisdom was completely valid: people who stuck together *survived*. They protected one another, provided for one another, looked after one another's children, and kept each other warm at night. And, by forming these groups, we began to create social bonds too: we told stories, we shared emotions, we gossiped. This connection led to a level of intimacy, deepening our bonds with one another out of empathy for the shared narratives. With that, the stakes for survival and our desire to protect one another only grew. Even though we've come a long way from those hunting and gathering days, it's still just as crucial that we find our tribe—maybe not to survive, but definitely to thrive. Nurturing a connection with people who make us feel safe, seen, and supported is vital, especially in such a fast-paced world that can be as isolating as it is overwhelming. Your tribe can look any way you want it to, whether it's a ragtag collection of friends-turned-family, actual family, or anyone else in your life who inspires you. The important thing is that you make time for them, which in turn will help you feel more rooted and content. Creating a celebration practice is the perfect way to do just that.

JUST LIKE ANY other kind of practice—mindfulness, spiritual, movement—a celebration practice supports your overall wellness. And just like these other types of practices, making a point to regularly gather helps you fine-tune in order to reap maximum benefits, like feeling happier, more purposeful, and more satisfied with your life. So don't just reserve gatherings for birthdays and holidays (though those are super-important too); think about all the other good stuff that deserves some special attention, no matter how small: have people over to plant some flowers in honor of the start of spring, put on a giant pot of pasta so everyone can

> Nurturing a connection with people who make us feel safe, seen, and supported is vital, especially in such a fast-paced world that can be as isolating as it is overwhelming.

help you carbo-load the night before you run your first 5K, get your witchy ladies together to gaze at the full moon and share your hopes and goals for the month to come, or host a casual potluck because it's Thursday, and you know what? Thursdays are awesome. Think about how much more good stuff you'd invite into your life if you stopped and celebrated those things! So let's get down to how you can make this practice a part of your life in the name of gratitude and good vibes.

Reasons to Have a Party . . .

TO FEEL PRETTY CONNECTED

Researchers now know that hanging out in groups—and moving rhythmically together, a.k.a. dancing—was how our ancestors would bond and communicate.[1] It wasn't just to knock a couple back and catch up on gossip; it was also crucial to making things work as a species—namely because it helped fellow tribemates identify who would make a nice, strong, healthy mate. Plus, they gave each other physical and emotional comfort, while also protecting one another from not-so-friendly groups or animals. They helped one another feel like they were part of something bigger than themselves, while also making the world seem a little safer and more forgiving. And, of course, there was also the perk of being able to make lots of new little humans. It's no wonder that we evolved to have "social brains," or neurological wiring that actually boosts our ability to play nice with others. That's thanks to the neocortex, the outermost layer of the brain, which is responsible for things like language, empathy, and emotional and behavioral regulation—all super-important skills when it comes to building and maintaining relationships. Unlike primates or other mammals, we're essentially programmed to tune in to—and care about—the thoughts and feelings of other people.[2] Even though we're no longer in danger of being gobbled up whole by some prehistoric beast, our brains haven't exactly caught up, so we're still rewarded for seeking the company of others. While researchers don't know exactly *how*, there are some who believe it's because we get a nice, juicy hit of feel-good dopamine when we engage in social behavior. But whether it's chemical or learned, we humans know a good thing when we see it, which is why the party's been going on ever since it moved out of the cave, setting the stage for how we gather now. Ancient Romans had festivals to honor their gods, including celebrations that eventually became Valentine's Day and Christmas. The Greeks offered up moon-shaped cakes to the moon goddess Artemis as a tribute and studded them with lit candles for a glowing effect—happy birthday, anyone? The Egyptians would come together to share music and good eats for the "Opening of the Year," as well as to reflect on the past and focus on their resolutions for the new year—champagne optional, I'm sure. And then there were the pagans, who were no strangers to a good time. Their festivals marked the changing of the seasons, giving thanks for things like a bountiful harvest and the fertility of the land at the first signs of spring (a practice that was eventually named after the goddess Éostre). Their midwinter celebrations meant epic feasts, gift giving, and decorating their homes with wreaths of holly, ivy, mistletoe, and pine. Thanks to them— with a little help from other old-school religious rituals—many of us have gotten to continue with similar traditions in our own families.

TO FEEL PRETTY GOOD

When we let our hair down in the name of a good time, we're also benefiting our bodies and minds. Strong personal relationships can influence our long-term health just as powerfully as getting enough sleep, eating nourishing foods, and not smoking. In fact, dozens of studies have shown that people with rooted connections to a tribe—friends or family—are happier, have fewer health problems, and live longer.[3] Social interaction has a positive impact on memory and cognitive function, making getting together one of the most important tools (along with diet and exercise) that we have to decrease our risk of Alzheimer's and dementia as we age.[4] People who make celebration a regular practice in order to express gratitude have more energy and less stress and anxiety, are more likely to help others, exercise more frequently, sleep better, have superior physical health, and are more likely to reach their goals.[5]

On the other hand, *lack* of social interaction can have a detrimental effect on our well-being.[6]

Scientists still aren't quite sure *why* we get such a boost from strong relationships, but it's suspected that it has something to do with triggering the release of stress-reducing hormones, which remedies the toxic effect that stress can have on everything from heart health to gut function to the immune system.[7] We also know that truly enjoying ourselves releases endorphins—our body's nourishing equivalent of going for a run or doing a sun salutation series—which gives us an overall sense of well-being, boosts our energy and vitality, and keeps us feeling young. It improves our relationships and connections with other people, which in turn helps ward off stress and depression.

This is not a free ticket to go overboard, however. Remember, there is a big difference between true connection and communication and what hap-

A party without a
cake is just a meeting.

—Julia Child

What do I want to celebrate?

What about this day/occasion/person do I love the most?

What feeling do I most want to convey with this event?

Do I want to fill my house with people or keep it to a few close friends?

What feels realistic for me? Do I want to set up and cook myself or do I delegate?

Do I keep things light and guilt-free or do I go decadent and indulgent?

What time of day feels right for this event?

Do I want to cap the festivities at a couple of hours or see how the event unfolds?

Do I want to serve alcohol at this event or not?

STEP 2: FINE-TUNE YOUR IDEA

There's no shortage of options when it comes to party concepts. The more personalized and customized you make them, the easier they are to plan and the more genuine they feel. These are just a few ideas to get you started. Using your answers to the *Drawing Board* prompts opposite as a guide, try picking an option from each column to see what you end up with!

STEP 3: DO IT RIGHT, DO IT LIGHT, OR DO IT EASY?

When planning a party, don't forget about real life. Moods shift, diets change, and time just never seems abundant enough. Instead of worrying that a guest's/your new nutritional regimen will get in the way of a good time, opt for

REASON TO CELEBRATE
(choose one)

- ○ Milestone birthday
- ○ Anniversary
- ○ Award-show viewing
- ○ Just because
- ○ Bachelor/ bachelorette
- ○ Bridal shower
- ○ Binge-watching the new season of a show (e.g., *Stranger Things*)
- ○ New moon/full moon
- ○ Big game
- ○ Horror movie marathon
- ○ Baby shower
- ○ Classic holiday
- ○ Child's birthday
- ○ Adult's birthday (e.g., You're fifty and fab!)
- ○ Olympics
- ○ Days of the week— Mondays don't have to be terrible; make them magical instead!
- ○ School starting/ ending
- ○ Housewarming
- ○ New job/promotion
- ○ It's raining!
- ○ It's sunny!

MOOD
(choose one)

- ○ Blissful
- ○ Cozy
- ○ Relaxed
- ○ Crazy
- ○ Devious
- ○ Sexy
- ○ Dark
- ○ Silly
- ○ Flirty
- ○ Funny
- ○ Thankful
- ○ Weird
- ○ Geeky
- ○ Meditative—gather your closest for some calm, quiet time
- ○ Romantic
- ○ Mellow
- ○ Naughty

THEME
(choose one)

- ○ Animals
- ○ Book or movie—try a *Great Gatsby* party!
- ○ Color
- ○ Zodiac sign
- ○ Fantasy
- ○ Favorite things
- ○ Fictional characters
- ○ Flowers/the garden—celebrate sunflowers
- ○ Food and drink
- ○ Games/trivia
- ○ Geographic location—go to Greece for an afternoon
- ○ Iconic eras
- ○ Masquerade/dress-up
- ○ Music
- ○ Number/letter of the alphabet
- ○ Seasons
- ○ Spa day
- ○ Sports
- ○ Things that go
- ○ Travel
- ○ Weather

TIME OF DAY
(choose one)

- ○ Early morning
- ○ Morning/breakfast
- ○ Early afternoon/ brunch
- ○ Afternoon/lunch
- ○ Late afternoon— perfect for catching fireflies and making s'mores
- ○ Early evening
- ○ Evening/dinner
- ○ Late night

updated, more healthful versions of some offerings—even party classics like meatballs and chili can get a veg-centric makeover. Instead of sweating over whether you'll have enough time/money/energy to go all out on every single detail, think about what you can simplify, delegate, or just forget altogether. A simple pot of stew can get all dressed up with a pretty pot, an arrangement of store-bought toppings in cute containers, and a loaf of good, crusty bread; a meal for a crowd is a cinch if everyone brings favorite childhood eats (instant conversation starter!); and *no one* will miss fancy-pants place settings at a dinner party, believe me. That said, if you're super revved up about going all in on a sophisticated party and want to tend to every last detail, then honor that! Throughout this book you'll see these different options when it comes to things like décor, favors, food, and drinks:

Do It Right means going the extra mile, whether it's a super-decadent twist on the menu, completely transforming a space with your décor, opting for favors that call for an extra trip to the party goods store, or getting down with DIY. What it does *not* mean is spending a lot of money or that you're doing it "wrong" if you choose to go a simpler route.

Do It Light means offering more healthful alternatives to the usual party noshes. It can be as simple as baking your veggie pancakes for brunch instead of frying them or offering smoothies instead of milkshakes.

Do It Easy means just that: EASY. It's looking to friends for help. It's saying *yes* when someone asks if they can bring something and saying *no* to spending all day in the kitchen before everyone arrives, so you are exhausted by the time the party starts, or being chained to the grill while your guests have all the fun. It means turning your dining room table into a giant meat and cheese board full of store-bought options or letting guests make their own salads from a selection of mix-ins and dressings—both are great examples of doing it easy. Trust me, easy can be just as polished and festive as doing it right.

A Formal Note on Formal

I'm all for setting a beautiful table and inviting friends over for an elegant dinner party. But, more often than not, I do not have the time to fuss over formality. And somehow that always translates to being more accessible. And for me it seems to work, becauseI never want my friends to feel like they can't have a good time because they're afraid to chip a plate or stain a tablecloth. I want people to feel like they can let loose, put their elbows on the table, maybe even get a little silly. It's all about leaving the outside world behind when they step through the door. If a party gets too *Downton Abbey*—and not in the good way—then it doesn't matter how beautiful the décor or your intentions are. You can put together the most lavish party, but if you don't create an environment where people feel comfortable enough to sit down and strike up a conversation with a stranger, then fun might be harder to come by. One trick I love for keeping things loose is mixing high and low: serving pizza on fine china, chili in an elegant copper pot, beer in crystal champagne glasses, or champagne in pretty plastic tumblers. Remember that polished is not the same thing as prim and proper.

When Parties Just Happen

Not all parties need a save the date or weeks of prep. Some of my favorite get-togethers are the ones where friends just happened to end up at my place. One example is New Year's Eve 2014, when I didn't feel like going out or doing anything and just wanted to be home. Over the course of the day, friends called to see what I was doing that night. I told them that I'd just be hanging out in my sweatpants, and if they asked if they could join, I said, "Sure!" Fast-forward to a few hours later when ten people were at my house, lounging in their pj's, drinking cocktails, and pretty much having the best time. We turned on some music, started singing and dancing, and just before it was time to watch the ball drop, we wrote down our wishes for the next year and burned them in the fireplace. It's one of my fondest memories, and it all started with "Yes, come over; I'll figure it out."

Some of my favorite get-togethers are the ones where friends just happened to end up at my place.

That's why I've included some of my favorite ideas for spur-of-the-moment pop-up parties here too. They really get to the heart of the Pretty Fun philosophy and highlight the importance of gathering, because if you can have a party on the fly, you know you have your celebration practice well honed. They're easy ways to seize a moment without worrying too much about having the perfect decorations or food. It's also why I'm a big fan of a Pretty Stocked Pantry (page 200), or having a kitchen loaded with just-in-case provisions that can be whipped up into a last-minute meal or put out as snacks. This way you can focus on what matters—the company!

Family Dinners Are Gatherings Too

I believe one of the most important things you can do as a parent is set aside time for the family to gather as its own special unit. It's a ritual that's been a part of my life from the very beginning, whether it was my gram filling our bellies with Jewish staples like brisket and matzoh ball soup, or the dinners that my parents would put together every chance they could. Now, in my own house, I try to make it happen at least twice a week, because it's a sacred time when we can share the intention of togetherness. We talk about what's going on in our lives or what happened that day, and just *be*. Something I really like to do with my kids is say grace. It's not a religious thing, just a gratitude thing—for our family, for our health, for everything we've been able to have. And then the conversation flows; we just *talk*.

What I've found is that if I have a busy week or a little too much time passes between these family meals, one of the kids will usually pipe up with "Mommy, we haven't had one of our dinners." That's when you realize they love it too and the time you spend together is beyond priceless—even if it's takeout and you put it on the nice plates. I like going the extra mile of having it feel special, but the most special thing is shutting everything off but one another.

For us, that starts with turning off all electronics. There are certain nonnegotiables in my house and that's one of them—no compromise, no arguing—it's never gonna happen; you're never going to convince me that you can use your phone at the dinner table when we're all eating together. The only exception is music, with the rule that if everyone can't agree on what to listen to, Mom chooses.

And everyone gets a job! There's usually something that your child can do, even if it's as small as finding the butter in the fridge or picking flowers for the table. It makes kids feel so proud to see how their efforts help make this a special thing for everyone. I try to make it fun and funny too, so no one feels like it's work. Sometimes I'll turn dinner chores into a game—whoever sets the table the neatest doesn't have to clean up! Then after the kids cover all the basics, I come in and fluff it up and make it look pretty. And yes, that includes using the china or the good plates—the nice stuff. I let my kids know that we are having a special night and that I trust them with things that are valuable to me. Because they're special and valuable to me too—and way more so!

No matter how little time we have, making the extra effort goes a long way with kids. Even if they don't seem to appreciate it now, they'll appreciate it down the road. (And chances are they do totally love it now, even if they have a funny way of showing it.) Not to mention the fact that research has shown that sharing a family meal has a positive impact on everything from grades, behavior, and self-esteem to lower rates of teen pregnancy, substance abuse, and eating or mood disorders.[8] Creating a space where children can tell stories gives them a chance to express their thoughts and feelings, which is associated with a greater sense of well-being. Gathering as a family is as holistic and healing a practice as any other—good for the body, the soul, and the mind. That's why throughout this book you'll find my suggestions for different ways to put together your own family dinners, whether it's DIY kebabs or the simplest roasted chicken of all time, a hump-day respite from a busy week or a lazy Sunday dinner with nowhere to rush off to.

Ways to get your kids involved with dinner prep:

* Have them gather ingredients or put them away

* Teach them how to pick fresh herbs from the stems

* Send them outside to collect items to decorate the table: stones, flowers, branches, etc.

* Show them how to set the table

* Get a child-friendly stepstool so they can watch as you chop, mix, etc.

* Depending on your child and your comfort level, even toddlers can get in on the cooking action with the right guidance using mixing spoons, whisks, and child-safe peelers and knives

Conversation starters with kids:

Here are just a few to get you started. For *tons* more that you can tailor to the specific ages of your children, go to the Family Dinner Project website (thefamilydinnerproject.org). It's an amazing organization that helps families connect over the dinner table.

* What's the funniest thing that happened to you today?

* What was the most challenging part of today?

* What are two things you felt grateful for this week?

* If you were a season, which season would you be and why?

* What should we do this weekend?

CHAPTER TWO

PRETTY FUN PLANNING BASICS

YOU'VE GOT THE intention; you've got the theme—and you've created the Pinterest board to prove it. But you can't go all in with the festivities without first nailing down a *plan*, from the budget to the menu. I know that sounds like taking the *fun* out of *Pretty Fun*, but trust me—tending to details early and keeping them in mind throughout the process will save headaches before, during, and after the party. If you're going to have a headache, let it be from not getting enough sleep because you were too busy dancing!

Budget Basics

Determining your budget first will help make sure that your party costs won't go to a scary place. Set a firm number as your ceiling, then make your goal about 20 percent below that to allow for last-minute additions. Remember that a fun party is not the same as an expensive one. Some of my favorite gatherings were ones where I spent almost nothing at all— it's the company that counts! And creativity goes much further—and feels way more special—than a bunch of stuff you paid a ton for. Also think about where you want to splurge and where you can save. You might have a full bar at New Year's (a must, if you ask me), but if a guest asks what to bring, say, "Champagne!" It's one less bottle for you to buy. Or have your guests bring a favorite dessert. Your game night doesn't need expensive decorations, so maybe shell out for a box of tacos from your favorite neighborhood spot.

Keeping Track of Expenses

For me, the easiest way to stay on budget is to keep a running list of where the money's going. Some people will tell you to estimate X percent for alcohol or Y percent for food, but because each party is different, there's no right or wrong way to budget. Use the worksheet below to get a sense of what kind of expenses your party might entail and where you might be able to save, then log your spending to help you stay on track.

cheap tricks:

* **Butcher paper.** Use this instead of table linens and just add markers to let guests write personalized messages.

* **Fabric store treasures.** Fabric by the yard can look lux as a tablecloth or draped over less-than-pretty furniture. Just measure the length and width of your table, then add how much "drop" you

	WHAT I NEED	HOW I SAVE
INVITATIONS	Depends on guest list. Will you also be sending save the dates first?	Go for an electronic invitation instead of splurging on stationery. I love Paperless Post or just send a quick email. That always works!
SET UP/RENTALS	Table linens, furniture (tables and chairs), tent, heaters, etc.	Ask friends or neighbors to borrow extra chairs and tables, or even a nearby restaurant. And if the weather might be inclement, put together an indoor Plan B instead of splurging on a tent or heaters. Also, see Cheap Tricks (pages 32 and 35).
DÉCOR	Balloons, wall hangings, streamers, flowers, candles, string lights, table accents, etc.	Butcher paper and markers instead of linens; color coordinated paper plates, bowls, and cups instead of dishes; single color candies in glass jars.
FOOD	Appetizers and snacks, main dish, sides, and something sweet, along with serving dishes, plates and utensils.	Dress up inexpensive store-bought dips and herbed olives in pretty serving bowls. Make one main dish and ask guests to bring sides, or make the whole affair a potluck and just provide beverages.
DRINKS	Bar (alcohol, mixers, and garnishes), nonalcoholic beverages (sodas, juices, and sparkling water), coffee and/or tea, ice, cups, etc.	Scale back the bar to one kind of alcohol or just serve your favorite beer or wine. Asking guests to bring their preferred beverages is also perfectly acceptable.
ENTERTAINMENT	DJ/band/sound system, magician, tarot reader, balloon artist, petting zoo, etc.	Put together your own playlist, or better yet, have guests submit their requests. Instead of renting expensive speakers, invest in a small set that connects to your phone or laptop—or see if someone coming to the party would be willing to bring theirs.

an invitation to getting your invites right

who: Go back to the *Drawing Board* prompts on page 20 to get a sense of whether you're vibing a small, intimate gathering or a big blowout. Also, know your friends—do you always have a few flaky no-shows or are there always a bunch of unexpected appearances? Use that to gauge how many people to ultimately invite.

what: I love the idea of picking out sweet stationery that ties in perfectly with my party's theme, but honestly, I'm terrible at invitations. It's hard to keep up with current addresses, and while I hate to admit it, I sometimes—accidentally!—leave people out. Plus, it's another expense that I could be putting toward the party itself. That's why I love, love, *love* Paperless Post, even for the smallest parties. My brother Oliver is always teasing me about it, because I'll send a Paperless Post for pretty much any occasion, like the most casual family dinner. It's seriously the best—there are supercute designs; you can save all your friends' e-mails so you'll never leave anyone out; you can easily send out mass updates, which means you can get the save the dates out early before all the details are nailed down;

and your guests are a lot more likely to RSVP. Such a win!

when: I'm all for keeping things spontaneous, but I feel the calmest about party planning when I can send a save the date as a heads-up, at least three to six weeks in advance. As far as when to have a party, go back to your *Drawing Board*. Do you want people out of your house by 11:30 P.M., midnight at the latest? Get things started around 6:00 or 6:30 P.M. Want to let the night just unfold? Set a start time of 8:30 P.M. and assume you'll have one wave of people coming on the earlier side and then another late-night crew who might be down to stay all night. Daytime parties should be more structured in terms of a start and end time, so people know how to plan their day and don't feel weird about leaving.

why: Think of your invitation as another tool in your intention toolbox. Use it to set the mood, establish the theme, or let guests know whether there's anything they should bring, wear, come prepared with, give thought to, etc. Invitations are the first glimpse your guests get of what you have in store for them!

want (how much fabric you want hanging over the side). General rules of thumb: 6 to 8 inches for casual, 15 inches for formal, and pooling on the floor for *draamaaa*.

✴ **Colorful paper tableware.** A simple palette that's coordinated with the rest of the theme will feel polished. Party goods stores and discount stores often have fun patterned options that can look chic when tied into a color scheme, or check out Etsy for really unique takes on all things disposable.

✴ **Buddy up.** Enlist friends to bring food or alcohol, tend bar, play live music, and help clean up afterward.

✴ **Grocery store bouquets.** Break up inexpensive (and maybe not-so-cute) arrangements into individual bud vases (or mason jars, pitchers, milk jars—whatever you have) to get more mileage and a chic, modern look, or lay a flower at each place setting for a romantic feel. Daisies, spray roses, and tulips are all great low-cost options here.

✴ **Score at the discount store.** Look for items that tie into the party's main theme and colors to avoid things feeling hodgepodge.

Food and Drink Basics

For me, having a party doesn't mean getting stuck in the kitchen all night just so I can serve up the most perfect dinner party (unless you count taco night, in which case, I'm all about stove duty!). Instead, I try to keep things as simple as possible so I can enjoy myself as much as my guests do. Here are some of my approaches.

Pretty Fun party food philosophies:

✳ **Think of your theme.** Food is one of the easiest ways to highlight the vibe of a party, whether it's charming (mini-churros for a Day of the Dead Fiesta) or cheeky (chocolate-dipped frozen bananas for your bestie's bachelorette).

✳ **Mix homemade with store-bought.** Pick a recipe or two for a made-with-love feel, then buy the rest. Elevate grocery store additions by transferring them to cute containers and plates. Dips like hummus, tzatziki, white bean spread, and tapenade go a long way with veg and crackers; marinated olives and spiced nuts are perfect for grazing; and everybody loves a good chilled grain or veggie salad that you can pick up from the deli. For more ideas, see Pretty Stocked Pantry (page 200).

✳ **Dig DIY.** Create a big spread so guests can mix and match to their taste or diet. Do it up right by decorating the table with mood-setting touches to make the food a visual focal point, whether it's traditional (flowers, candles) or theme-related party goods (ref whistles for a football Sunday, tiny trophies filled with candies for a backyard sports tournament, marshmallow snowmen for a cozy wintertime gathering).

Figure out one signature dish that you can make so incredibly well that everyone will start salivating for it the moment they see your invitation.

* **Stock up on snacks.** You can never go wrong with lots of nibbles (nuts, popcorn, pretzels, chocolate candies) and spreading them around a party. People tend to flow where the food is. Nothing says "Sit here!" more than a little bowl of olives with a dish for pits on a table next to a comfy chair.

* **Don't hesitate to ask.** Whether you're just saying the magic word ("Yes!") to guests who ask whether they can bring anything or asking people to BYO (beer, picnic side, ice, dessert, you name it), getting a hand with food and drinks—or anything else, for that matter—is not only helpful, but it also makes your guests feel like they helped make the party great.

* **Find your signature.** You don't have to start from scratch with a new concept every time you have people over, at least when it comes to food. Figure out one signature dish that you can make so incredibly well that everyone will start salivating for it the moment they see your invitation. Think about touches that are unique to you—maybe they're a reflection of where you grew up or where your family's from. I love making my guests feel right at home with one of the dishes I grew up eating from my mom's heritage mash-up of Hungarian Jewish and Southern Baptist, or going all in with a traditional bagel schmearfest.

THE BAR

The only rule for stocking a bar is to make sure there's a little something for everyone. Below are my three takes on this important celebration setup.

Do It Right: Two words: "full bar." New Year's Eve, the major holidays, and anything else more formal and festive call for all libations on deck. Con-

sider having a selection of elements that you can tailor to your event and your guests' tastes. Revisit your *Drawing Board* to get clarity on how you can reinforce the intention of the gathering.

- ✳ **The hard stuff:** gin, vodka, whiskey or bourbon, and tequila are classic stand-bys that can be the foundation for a number of cocktail variations. You could also change things up with a more curated selection, like an assortment of rums (light, aged, spiced) for a tropical or warm-weather vibe. Or think about a flight of bourbons, which work for setting a cozy mood (think Old Fashioneds or sipping from tumblers while huddling around the fire) or for a lighter, brighter affair (Mint Juleps for the Kentucky Derby!). I also love to throw in something unexpected that people may not have tried before like Scandinavian *Brännvin*, Italian Grappa, or French Calvados.

- ✳ **The mixers:** Build a foundation with club soda and/or tonic and a few juices (lemon, lime, cranberry, orange, grapefruit, tomato, pineapple, mango, pomegranate). Then throw in an unexpected twist: infused simple syrups (check out jalapeño on page 223 or ginger-thyme on page 92), tea (chai, matcha, black, hibiscus—search online for any number of fun tea-based cocktails), even cold-pressed green juice—plus a splash of tequila, agave, and lime juice for good measure.

- ✳ **The garnishes:** You can't go wrong with the classics (limes, lemons, olives), but you can also punch things up with boozy fruit (peaches, cherries, or berries soaked in your favorite spirit), blue cheese-stuffed olives, infused sugars for coating glass rims (fill a small jar with cane or coconut sugar, add flavor element of choice—dried edible lavender, chili powder, cardamom—and just let sit for 1 to 2 weeks), or ice cubes studded with pretty fresh herbs or edible flowers.

- ✳ **The splurges:** Liqueurs and bitters offer even more options to play around with and can be stirred into cocktails or sipped straight over ice. There's the bright botanicals like Campari, Aperol, Cynar, Fernet-Branca, and vermouth; the deep-flavored fruits (chambord, crème de cassis, cherry heering); and the richly sweet (amaretto, frangelico, crème de cacao).

* **The wines:** At the very least, aim for something white, something red, and something sparkling. When choosing wines, think about what food you're serving, the season, and of course, your personal preference. Ask an expert at your local wine shop to make suggestions, and maybe even have her steer you towards lesser known varietals like a Mencia from Spain or wines from unexpected places like Croatia or Greece, or change things up by serving an orange wine instead of the usual rosé.

* **The beers:** Beers tend to fall in one of three categories: aromatic, hoppy ales; smooth, refreshing lagers; and dark, rich stouts. Lagers are going to be your go-to crowd pleaser (like Stella Artois or Corona); ales tend to be especially tasty with food; and stouts go best with richer, smokier fare (think big roasts or grilled meats). Put together a selection of one down-the-middle option plus one or two fun things to try. Explore craft breweries in your area—small-batch producers who put a lot of heart and soul into their flavors and techniques—or transport your guests with regional options like a flight of Japanese, German, or Belgian beers.

Do It Light: If you want to offer drinks beyond just the standard sodas and bottled water, but want to skip the alcohol, consider:

* **A signature mocktail:** Just about any fresh juice plus seltzer makes a tasty spritzer—orange, grapefruit, mango, peach—and you can add a small spoonful of infused simple syrup for an even more complex flavor. Try a nonalcoholic version of the Grapefruit-Jalapeño Mezcal Punch on page 223 or Ginger-Thyme Margaritas on page 92.

Drink when you are happy, but never because you are miserable.

—G.K. Chesterton

* **Organic sodas and juices:** These lower-sugar, nonartificial options are particularly great if you're having a lot of kids over. Some of my favorites are Virgil's Root Beer, Oogavé sodas, HotLips Real Fruit Soda, and Fizzy Lizzy sodas, along with Back to Nature, Honest Kids, and Whole Foods 365 juices.

* **Tea:** An underrated beverage option, especially for lending a calming element to more intimate gatherings. I like having a selection to offer, so there's something for everyone, whether it's traditional black, green, or oolong; soothing chamomile, jasmine, or mint; or something fun and interesting (and very healing) like ginger-turmeric, sage, or kukicha.

Do It Easy: For the times when a full bar isn't necessary, appropriate, or affordable:

* Focus on one kind of beverage and riff on that. Or maybe it's just wine or beer on offer, or tequila, tequila, tequila (just add salt and limes!).

* Ask guests to bring the drinks they love the most: done and done.

A WORD ON ICE

You can *never* have too much ice at a party. It's always the first thing to run out, and there's no bigger bummer than lukewarm drinks. Don't rely on the stuff your freezer makes; invest in at least a couple of bags more and either clear out a big old section of your freezer or buy/borrow a cooler.

Pretty Fun Party Rules: To Sum It Up

Now that you have the basics covered—your intention set, theme chosen, invitations sent, menu planned, and bar stocked—here are the rules to follow for an event to remember:

✳ **Party Rule #1:** *Know why you are having it!*

Stay true to your intention in order to create a cohesive-feeling party that encourages connection among your guests. Stick with what's comfortable and makes you feel good. Don't make your party a certain way because you think you're supposed to.

✳ **Party Rule #2:** *Focus on what really matters to you; don't worry about the rest.*

You don't have to do it all to prove something—there's definitely no award for hardest-working host! Choose a few key things to do yourself and outsource the rest. And remember that there's absolutely no shame in the store-bought or disposable. Don't get caught up in the "right" details just because you think people will appreciate how much money you've spent. If you can't afford the party you want, financially or energetically, change it up to suit. The more pressure you put on yourself, the more apt you are to question Rule #1 and break Rule #7, the most crucial of the bunch.

✳ **Party Rule #3:** *Always say yes!*

I've said it about a billion times already, but that's because it's a really important rule! If someone asks if they can bring something, the answer is *always* yes. Whether it's their favorite beer or whiskey, something sparkling for an occasion that calls for it, something sweet for a dinner

If we are ever to enjoy life, now is the time—not tomorrow, nor next year . . . Today should always be our most wonderful day.

—Thomas Dreier

you're making but don't have time to pull together a dessert—it's always a good idea to let people chip in. If someone asks if they can help, again, Y-E-S. Putting out plates and silverware, making sure everyone has a drink, lighting candles, refreshing the ice, letting everyone know dinner is ready—delegation is key to a low-stress party.

* **Party Rule #4:** *Have a little something prepared to say to your guests.*

One of the best ways to get everyone feeling all the good feelings at a party—no matter how silly a gathering it is—is to say a little something. If it's a smaller gathering, like during the holidays or a family dinner, have everyone share. Maybe it's something they're grateful for, something they're ready to let go of, something they love most about the guest of honor, or something great that happened to them that day. And no matter the occasion, I think the host should always say something to her guests, whether it's a toast, some thoughts on why you're gathering that day, or just a simple "Thank you all for coming." After all your guests have arrived and settled—usually about forty minutes to an hour in, or after the first course if it's a more formal dinner—clink a glass and share a few words. Everybody loves those moments.

* **Party Rule #5:** *Forget the mess.*

Some people have a hard time with the idea of their house getting dirty. I get it. But if you're going to entertain, that just has to go out the window. Know this; embrace this: Your house is going to get dirty and you'll probably end up cleaning most of it. And that's fine. It's not the end of the world! If you're truly having a tough time letting go and you can afford it, hire someone to come the next morning. But even the biggest, most out-of-hand parties don't take three days to clean up after. It's usually only a few hours. And while I'd never ask my guests to help, it's always fun to see who are the last people left gathering up empty cups and swabbing down tables. Those are usually the people with whom you are the closest, or the new friends you are happiest to have made, and honestly, it ends up being my favorite time of the night. There's also something a little naughty about leaving it all for the morning—when you wake up and see the proof that everyone had a great time the night before. Not for the faint of heart, though!

✶ **Party Rule #6:** *Put it in writing.*

There's nothing lovelier than a handwritten note. Take the time to thank people for coming to your party, especially if they brought something or helped in any other way. Maybe even add a detail about something they said or did that was funny or otherwise memorable, since it creates even more connection. That said, this is where I oftentimes fall short. Considering I keep all my contacts filed away in Paperless Post so I don't forget to invite anyone, I don't exactly have a great handwritten track record. And I recognize that with everything going on in the day, taking the time to write everyone a card isn't exactly easy. But if you can, it's one of the nicest, most thoughtful touches, and it makes people feel so special.

✶ **Party Rule #7:** *The host should be having the most fun!*

I've saved the most important rule for last, so hear this now: *You* should be having the most fun at your party. From the second the party starts, you should make it a point to enjoy and to let anything else go. You've done all the prep, made all the smart decisions (as in, not making crepes to order all night), and now it's time to enjoy the fruits of your labor. And if something goes wrong—people leave early, you burn dinner, the night is a total and utter disaster—it doesn't matter; stay in the moment. If you're happy and having a blast, everyone else will be too.

PART TWO

PRETTY EXCITED!

WINTER

Holiday Cookie Bake-Off

I go all in when it comes to the holidays. From the weekend after Thanksgiving to New Year's Day, my house is decorated to the hilt: tons of garlands and wreaths and all the decorations that I've been collecting almost my whole life, ranging from the super-traditional greens and reds to clean and modern silvers and whites. And there's always a festive playlist on rotation, from Frank Sinatra to Michael Bublé. So when it comes to a holiday party, I want my guests to be swimming in seasonal cheer. I usually host a Christmas Eve gathering that starts around 5:00 or 5:30 P.M., so the kids and adults can celebrate together. Then as the kids go off to bed, the adults can linger. And while I've been known to require that everyone sings carols together (complete with lyric sheets—a holdover from my parents' amazing holiday parties), one of the most fun things I've done over the years is have a proper bake-off. Usually it's cookies, but it could be bars, pies, bread, cakes, you name it. Basically, everyone brings their signature confections and dresses them up so they look supercute on the table. (One year I made my cookies look like ornaments and hung them all on a little

> I want my guests to be swimming in seasonal cheer.

tree with tiny wrapped presents underneath . . . filled with more cookies to give to everyone as favors! So over the top, so cute.) Then all the non-bakers rate them. No professional baking skills required, and no crazy, involved to-do list that usually comes with throwing a traditional holiday party, just a sense of humor and a sweet tooth.

Planning a Bake-off

1. **Fill in your guests on what to bring—cookies, pies, etc.** Make sure they know presentation counts! The more ridiculous, the better.

2. **Designate an area in your house**—your dining room table, a coffee table, sideboard, your kitchen island—to display the contenders.

3. **All non-bakers are welcome to be judges.** Agree on the judging criteria, anything from wow factor to yum factor.

4. **Share the running commentary.** If it's later in the night and everyone's had a few drinks—and it won't hurt any of the participants' feelings—invite the judges to voice their tasting notes for the audience.

5. **Tally the votes and crown the winner!** We don't usually do a prize, but if you want to get a special something for the best baker, go for it. In my opinion, something to be used in future baking projects is the perfect reward.

winning molten chocolate cookies

If there's one secret to securing a bake-off win, it's *chocolate*. These rich chocolate cookies, which are filled with even more ooey-gooey chocolate, are a shoe-in for first place. They're made with whole wheat flour, which has a slightly nuttier taste than all-purpose flour—and a bit more fiber (but no need to advertise).

In a large bowl, sift together the cocoa, flour, baking powder, cinnamon, and salt. Set aside.

In the bowl of a stand mixer fitted with the paddle attachment, or in a large bowl with a hand mixer or rubber spatula, beat the melted butter, granulated sugar, egg, and vanilla on low speed until well incorporated, about 1 minute. Add the dry ingredients and mix for another minute on low speed to combine. Use a wooden spoon or rubber spatula to fold in the nuts and chocolate chips. Transfer the bowl to the refrigerator to chill for 1 hour.

Preheat the oven to 350°F. Line a baking sheet with parchment paper or a silicone baking mat. Place about ¾ cup confectioners' sugar in a small bowl.

Form the dough into 1-inch balls and roll each in the confectioners' sugar to coat completely. Shake off any excess sugar and arrange the cookies on the prepared baking sheet about 1½ inches apart. Bake for 12 minutes, or until the cookies are puffed and the sugar has cracked apart. They will look underdone in the center—that's what you want! Let them sit for 5 minutes, then transfer the cookies to a wire rack to cool completely. Store in a covered container at room temperature for 3 to 5 days, or in the freezer for up to 3 months.

MAKES ABOUT 22 COOKIES

3 tablespoons unsweetened cocoa, preferably Dutch-process

½ cup whole wheat flour

½ teaspoon baking powder

1 teaspoon ground cinnamon

⅛ teaspoon salt

3 tablespoons unsalted butter, melted

½ cup granulated sugar

1 large egg

½ teaspoon vanilla extract

¼ cup finely ground toasted hazelnuts

½ cup semisweet chocolate chips

Confectioners' sugar

Do It Easy

SERVE-YOURSELF STEW

Since the bake-off is the star of the show here, I keep the food simple for this kind of gathering—definitely no fussy sit-down situation, and definitely nothing that will keep me in the kitchen. When I want to go big on flavor while keeping things feeling homey and warm, I love putting out a big pot of stew: creamy white bean and sage; rich, heady beef bourguignon; bright, fresh cioppino; even elk (my mom's recipe!)—any of which you can find a great recipe for online (okay, maybe not the elk), and all of which are great for making ahead of time. They don't require more than a beautiful loaf of crusty bread. Presentation is everything: find a pretty enamel or copper pot for the stew and set it on a warmer. Arrange any toppings and condiments (grated cheese, olive oil, flaked salt, and pepper) in bowls or cruets, and go for real stuff (glasses, dishes, and silverware) instead of disposable.

Arrange any toppings and condiments for guests to help themselves:

- ✳ Grated or Crumbled Cheese (Parmesan, Pecorino, Goat, Feta)

- ✳ High-Quality Olive oil

- ✳ Finishing Vinegars like Moscatel, Balsamic, or Saba

- ✳ Flaky sea salt

- ✳ Fresh Herbs (nothing adds a pop of color like a sprinkle of chopped chives, parsley, or cilantro)

- ✳ Bread Crumbs or Croutons (just toss some roughly torn day-old bread in a pan with olive oil until golden; sprinkle with salt and done!)

- ✳ Toasted Nuts or Seeds (walnuts or pecans; pumpkin or sunflower seeds)

- ✳ Pickled Veggies (radishes, beets, mushrooms, fennel)

- ✳ Something Creamy, like Greek Yogurt, Creme Fraiche, or Sour Cream

baby, it's cold outside bar

There is something deeply satisfying about wrapping your hands around a steaming mug on a cold, dreary day. It reminds me of coming inside after playing in the snow, settling into a hot bath, and then changing into my comfiest, coziest pajamas. Memories like that are some of my fondest, and I love to recreate that for my kids—or any guests who have come over for a winter gathering. To capture that spirit, I set up a station with warm apple cider and hot chocolate and let everyone adorn their cups with tasty garnishes like:

- ✳ Cinnamon sticks or ground cinnamon

- ✳ Toasted marshmallows

- ✳ Chocolate shavings or sprinkles

- ✳ Candy canes

- ✳ Whipped cream

- ✳ Chopped nuts

- ✳ Baileys, bourbon, brandy, or Frangelico (for the adults)

- ✳ Chocolate wafers or cookies

- ✳ Miniature spice sachets, or small bits of cheesecloth wrapped around crushed cinnamon sticks, star anise, cloves, and cardamom pods

To make the table feel welcoming and seasonal, add natural décor like evergreen branches, pinecones, wreaths or garlands;

soft textural elements like knit or flannel trivets, runners, or napkins (especially in plaids or fair isle); or keep things simple and all-white with touches of silver and gold. Finish off the spread with sweet snacks like chocolate-dipped fruit (especially citrus); gingerbread cookies or ginger snaps; white chocolate-peppermint bark; spiced, roasted nuts; cinnamon-sugar doughnuts, or my favorite Greatest-Hits Pie (page 245).

Do It Right

HOLIDAY DÉCOR

First, pick your colors. Are you a retro red-and-green kind of girl? A modern hot-pink lady? Like classy all-white everything? If you're like me and deck the halls up to the brim, then look to your decorations for inspiration. Thread those colors through all the other elements of your party—napkins, tablecloths, runners—while also adding a few holiday-specific touches. Below are some elements that I love, especially for a focal-point table. A focal-point table is basically what it sounds like—a point in the room that not only catches the eye but tends to become the spot where people congregate. It's

MAKING MEMORIES

This time of year can be the stuff of kids' dreams. So many of my most cherished childhood moments came from the family time at the holidays. Remember to pause, even during all the December hustle and bustle, to make time for your littlest loved ones—one-on-one shopping trips, wrapping nights, cooking tasks, or just drinking cocoa on a frosty day. That's what they'll cherish.

usually where the food is arranged, though it could be the sweets table or where you've set up the bar. It's a great visual opportunity to create even more of an aesthetic or vibe that's unique to your gathering.

* Pinecones, especially in bowls with other textural elements

* Moss, antlers, and feathers—total enchanted forest vibes

* Any kind of mistletoe-y berries

* Tea lights

* Evergreen branches

* Holly, especially with white berries

* Candy canes or other seasonal candy

* Fresh herbs, especially rosemary, thyme, and sage

New Year's Eve

New Year's Eve isn't the time to reinvent the wheel. It's the time for getting all dressed up, for fun, for friends, and for tons of food and drink—definitely a full bar and loads of little nibbles to choose from versus a heavy, sleep-inducing meal. It's all about everybody being able to have exactly what they want. It's a full-on celebration of decadence and just the right amount of debauchery. This is a great place for taking people up on the offer to bring something—the more bubbly, the better!

But just because the night is all about having a good time doesn't mean you can't tie in a grounding element. As tradition tells us, New Year's is also a time for reflection, setting resolutions, and new beginnings.

Infusing Intention

* Set up a table with paper and pens where guests can write down something they want to let go of. After the countdown and the cheering and kissing are over, have everyone take a moment to put these items into the fire, or collect them in a pretty basket for you to discard on their behalf.

* Offer a selection of colorful strings and ask guests to enlist a friend to tie one on their wrist. Have them make a wish so when the string breaks, that hope will float into the universe and come true.

kumquat champagne cocktail

Another fun twist on the traditional champagne is adding a flavored syrup. I have a bunch of kumquat trees growing in my yard, and every year there is so much fruit that I have to figure out what to do with it all. I landed on this recipe, where you're essentially making a flavored simple syrup and adding it to champagne, plus a few slices of the fruit for garnish. I love that it's just the slightest bit bitter, so the whole situation doesn't become overly sweet. You could easily substitute another kind of citrus, such as blood orange, lemon, or grapefruit, if it's easier to find.

In a small saucepan, combine the sugar and kumquats with 1 cup water. Stir to dissolve the sugar and bring to a boil. Reduce the heat and simmer for 15 minutes. Remove the pot from the heat and cover. Let the syrup steep for 30 minutes. Strain the syrup into a container and let cool completely.

To serve, spoon 1 tablespoon syrup into a champagne flute and top with champagne or prosecco. Garnish with candied citrus peels or any of the garnishes mentioned in "A Turned-Up Toast" (page 68). Store any leftover syrup in the fridge for up to 1 month.

MAKES 12 COCKTAILS

1 cup sugar

1 cup kumquats, 2 oranges, or 1 grapefruit

2 bottles chilled champagne or prosecco

Candied citrus peels or other garnishes, optional

pretty good tip: To calculate how much champagne or sparkling wine you'll need for everyone to have at least one glass for a toast, figure that one 750ml bottle can fill five glasses.

A TURNED-UP TOAST

Nothing rings in the New Year—or marks a special occasion—more than a little sparkle. Make your flutes a little more festive with these sweet additions:

* Edible flowers
* Candied citrus rinds
* Gummy bears
* Raspberries or blackberries
* Pomegranate seeds
* Colored rock candy

Do It Right

ALL THE BOARDS

One of the best ways to feed a big group of people—and fortify them for a long night of celebrating—is to arrange one mega board piled high with all the meaty, salty, sweet, crunchy, and creamy indulgences that someone could possibly want. Here's how I like to do it:

* **Pick a large, centrally located surface, such as a dining room or kitchen table, kitchen island, or big side table.** Consider setting up a folding table (with a handsome tablecloth) if one of those won't work.

* **Make the table the party's visual focal point.** Add large trays and boards to display the food, especially ones in textural materials like wood,

marble, or slate. Then scatter in elements of varying heights, like cake stands. Keep things from feeling too precious with mismatched paring knives and spreaders. Then tie in the party's colors and theme using table linens, favors, or trinkets.

✴ **Select a variety of foods that tie together.** I don't like to limit myself to old-fashioned meat-and-cheese board combos; I like spreads that you don't normally see arranged across an entire table. Think of an Old Master still life with tons of German-style smoked meats (plus a vegan one or two) and exotic mustards, a raw bar with shrimp and oysters alongside creatively flavored mignonettes and dipping sauces (think, rosé mignonette and curried tartar sauce), or surf 'n' turf with a larger-than-life combination of the two, plus any kind of charcuterie or cheese you love. And don't forget about mini-bagels, smoked fish, and all the spreads! Or caviar and blini! See what your budget allows for and go for it.

✴ **Don't be embarrassed to ask for help—you're not a cheese/sausage/ seafood/condiment expert!** Say to your cheesemonger or deli guy or gal, "I'm having twenty people over. How much should I buy? What's a good variety?" They're in the foodstuffs business—it's what they do!

✴ **Keep it colorful.** Layer up the goods with pretty seasonal additions like pomegranate seeds, small apples and pears (especially if the leaves are still attached), and jewel-toned dried fruits (apricots, figs, cranberries) and jams. You'll also want plenty of breadsticks, crackers, nuts, and olives.

✴ **Don't spread things out too much; mound them up high.** You want the table to feel abundant and full. That said, keep the cheese and meat from touching. I'm just not into that.

Use a similar approach to your sweets board as you do for the savories—include varying heights and colors, make it feel abundant, and offer lots and lots of options. I don't know about you, but I don't think I'd feel right about myself if there weren't at least a selection of cookies, bars, or brownies; maybe a seasonal pie; some good quality dark chocolate, and of course lots of fresh fruit.

Do It Light

Crudités, or veggies with dip, is such a party standard, but it so often doesn't get the love it deserves. Offering an amped-up take on the usual carrots and celery sticks with ranch dressing is not only a fun way to add color to your spread, but also to offer a snack option that's nourishing for all the senses. I especially love including veggies that look like they just came from the ground—the more misshapen and craggy, the better. It makes them feel inviting and fresh, like little subliminal pleasure buttons. Oddly shaped veggies are not only just as nutrient-rich and delicious as their more attractive

A NEW FOCUS

New Year's Eve can be all about glitz, glamour, and over-the-top fun, but don't forget to use the evening as a time to reflect on the year that has passed and all that lies ahead. This is a night for making plans, embracing the idea of starting fresh the following day, and celebrating the support of those who will be by your side cheering you on.

cousins, but they also add personality to your table (not to mention that you're saving them from most likely becoming food waste).

Pile up a tray with tempting options like radishes, endive, fennel, kohlrabi, jicama, radicchio, sugar snap peas, or baby carrots with the greens still attached (especially the gorgeous red and purple varieties). Pair them with lighter dips and dressings like my vegan garden goddess (page 136), an herbed garlic spread, red pepper dip, pesto, or tapenade—store-bought is just fine!

DÉCOR

Tonight's the night to go a little wild, including with the decorations. I love a good theme for New Year's Eve (1920s *Great Gatsby*, Bonnie and Clyde); think sexy and cool—or at the very least stick with a color scheme. I'm always changing up my selections, but I like to stay in the metallic family. Then I layer in all the festive doodads like hats, tiaras, blowers, and sparklers and go wild.

Open-Door Football Sunday

If it's the winter and it's Sunday, everyone knows where I'm going to be all day and that they're welcome to drop in. They know there'll be food, the game will be on, and that all they need to do is put up their feet. It's what I call my open-door football Sundays. I'll put out a spread of essential game-day eats like wings and chili (with a sneaky Do It Light twist) and then let everyone fend for themselves. Football Sundays mean paper plates and napkins (or who are we kidding, paper towels) and keeping it *easy*. *Do* know that it's going to get crazy, because everyone will bring their kids and their dogs and your house is going to be a mess. *Don't* be afraid to get totally obnoxious and wear every single piece of clothing that represents your team. (Go Broncos!)

Do It Light

Simple swaps, like veggies for meat and baking instead of frying make these junk-food classics a little healthier. No one will know you messed with their sacred game-day snacks.

veggie chili

I used to think chili was a sad mix of beans and tomatoes. But this rich, hearty, smoky 'n' spicy version is on a whole other level and is delicious enough to hold its own on a party spread, but healthful enough to be in your weekday dinner rotation. Serve with tons of healthy toppings, like pickled jalapeños, cilantro, avocado, chopped onion or scallion, tortilla strips, and sliced radishes. Okay, and sour cream and bacon bits—just in case.

I like putting the pot of chili right on the table, either on a warmer or a trivet, and then letting people help themselves. If you don't love the way your pot looks, just transfer the chili to a large serving bowl with a ladle or big spoon, or set out a bunch of preportioned bowls on your table. A nice touch is including a handwritten sign that describes what's in the chili and invites your guests to load their bowls up as they please, along with smaller labels for each of the garnishes, so the spread is super user-friendly.

SERVES 8 TO 10

2 tablespoons extra virgin olive oil

4 garlic cloves, minced

1 medium yellow onion, diced

1 red bell pepper, seeded and diced

1 yellow bell pepper, seeded and diced

1 medium sweet potato or 2 medium carrots, peeled and diced

1½ teaspoons ground cumin

1 teaspoon chipotle chili powder

Kosher salt, to taste

Freshly ground black pepper, to taste

¾ cup (6 ounces) tomato paste

3 cups vegetable broth

One 15.5-ounce can black beans, drained and rinsed

One 15.5-ounce can pinto beans, drained and rinsed

One 14.5-ounce can diced tomatoes with green chilies, drained

One 14.5-ounce can diced tomatoes

veggie chili (continued)

One 7-ounce can chipotle
chilies in adobo sauce,
with the chilies chopped
and sauce reserved
2 limes, cut into wedges,
for serving

Heat the oil in a large pot over medium-high heat. Add the garlic, onion, bell peppers, and sweet potato or carrots and cook, stirring occasionally, until all the veggies start to soften and even get a little brown, 8 to 10 minutes. Add the cumin and chili powder, and season with salt and pepper. Cook until the spices are fragrant, about 1 minute. Stir in the tomato paste and cook, while continuing to stir, until the paste turns a deep red, 2 to 3 minutes.

Add the broth, beans, tomatoes, chipotle chilies, and reserved adobo sauce. Stir, making sure to scrape up all those yummy brown bits at the bottom of the pot, and bring to a boil. Reduce the heat to low and simmer for 30 minutes or until the liquid has reduced slightly. Adjust the seasoning to your liking and serve each bowl with a good squeeze of lime over the top.

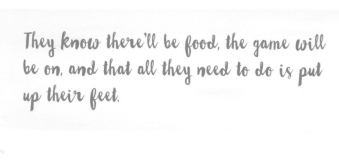

They know there'll be food, the game will be on, and that all they need to do is put up their feet.

crispy oven-baked buffalo wings

Frying is almost beside the point when you have Frank's RedHot sauce and butter. This baked version gets nice and crispy in the oven—without all the extra oil.

Preheat the oven to 400°F. Place wire racks on 2 large rimmed baking sheets and set aside.

In a large bowl, toss the chicken wings with the canola or vegetable oil, salt, and pepper until the wings are evenly coated. Divide the wings between the prepared baking sheets and make sure they're spread in a single layer and have a little room between them.

Bake for 45 to 50 minutes, until the wings are cooked through and the skin is golden and crispy.

Meanwhile, make the sauce. In a medium bowl, whisk together the butter and hot sauce. Season with salt and pepper to taste.

Toss the wings with the sauce, transfer them to your favorite platter, and serve 'em while they're hot—with plenty of napkins!

SERVES 4 TO 6

5 pounds chicken wings, tips removed and separated at the joint

2 tablespoons canola or vegetable oil

1 tablespoon kosher salt, plus more to taste

¾ teaspoon freshly ground black pepper, plus more to taste

2 tablespoons unsalted butter, melted

½ cup Frank's RedHot sauce or other hot sauce

Do It Easy

Today is not the day for any extra frills. Don't have time to cook? Order sandwiches from your favorite deli. Put out store-bought salsa and guacamole with chips and pretzels. Have a few footballs lying around—at least one real one and a couple of Nerf ones for the little guys—so everyone can stretch their legs between plays. Otherwise, don't worry about tending to anyone. If it's your team and a big game, it's definitely acceptable for this to be the one party where you don't worry about being the host. "Hey, is there food?" *Yeah, it's on the stove.* "Hey, do you have beer?" *Yeah, it's in the garage; help yourself.*

pretty fun tip: Gluten-free pretzels and grain-free tortilla chips taste just as good as the regular ones these days—put them in a bowl and no one will know the difference!

> ### GAME ON!
>
> I hope you enjoy your Sundays as much as I do. Root for your team, wear their colors, yell at the television, and argue with your friends over bad calls. You might just hear me screaming "Go Broncos!" from my house!

Do It Right

As a nice addition to the veggie chili and the oven-baked wings (easy and sooooo good), you might feel inclined to take it up a notch. The *one* thing to go the extra mile (more like quarter mile) for on football Sunday is drinks. Fill a big tub with ice and many types of beer. Even if you don't drink beer, there's going to be a bunch of people who do. And if someone asks what to bring—their favorite beer! I also like having a second tub with ice that I fill with cans of organic sodas, especially since it's the one day I'll let my kids have one.

Valentine's Day: Naughty and Nice

I devoted an entire section of *Pretty Happy* to rediscovering pleasure. I was referring to pleasure of all kinds, from the simple, silly ones, like going sledding or building a sand castle, to the biggie: sex. It is so important to celebrate our sexuality, and what a great day to do it! Our lives are so busy these days, and sex often gets pushed way down on the priority list. We're tired at the end of the day, and we jump out of bed in the morning because we have too much to do. But sex is such a deep connection, and it is part of our relationship with our partner that needs to be nurtured in a very special way.

That being said, your partner shouldn't be the only recipient of your affection on Valentine's Day. Make all the people you care most about your Valentine! Your parents, your children, your best friends should all feel the love that day. I love to give mushy cards to my tribe on February 14. I send flowers to single gal pals so they know I love them. And, remember, you don't have to wait for Valentine's Day—every day is a great day to show your people what they mean to you. Just a quick note, a small gift left in their mailbox, a text that lets them know you are thinking of them, a message tucked inside your child's lunchbox. That's the stuff strong connections are made of.

Now, for the sake of this book, I'm suggesting a more intimate Valentine's Day affair, one that has a distinctly sexy, adult feel. This holiday isn't so much about whipping up an elaborate meal as it is about setting the mood, whether it's sweet and playful or a little dark and mischievous. Either way, open your heart, let down your walls, and do it *right*. Here I've imagined two scenarios: one for day and one for night. Go to the **Drawing Board** to tune into what your intentions are for this day, reflect on the unique connection that you and your partner have, and give thought on how you want to celebrate it.

Daytime: A Little Nice

Do It Right

Valentine's morning is for doing the things you love most with your partner, even if it's just watching the news, teaming up on the crossword puzzle, or doing something small that makes you both laugh; it's a time for snuggling, nuzzling, and definitely treating yourselves to a sumptuous breakfast in bed—or maybe even in the bath.

Nighttime: A Lot Naughty

Do It Right

I don't think I need to spell out what Valentine's evening means for most of us. Leave the dishes in the sink, put the kids to bed, and turn off your cell phones. Put on some of your favorite sexy music. Light some candles. Close the blinds and lock the door. Maybe get the babysitter to take the kids out of the house all together so you can try to take things outside of the bedroom for a change! Break out those flavored whipped creams—but this time serve them on each other instead of in beautiful glass dishes!! If that feels too messy, try some of those naughty dice that are out there. Remember, tonight is all about giving and receiving pleasure—and creating intimate connection. But you can also have fun! Have you ever done a striptease for your partner? Worn a sexy costume? Tied a silky blindfold on him while you kissed him from head to toe? Head to the bathroom and fill the tub with sultry flowers, like black dahlias, hellebores, and black roses. Add sensual oils to the water that fill the room with sexy scents and slide in together for a warm, soothing embrace. Or, go for something completely silly and bring the kiddie pool inside, load it with rose petals, and roll around. That is sure to get you laughing, and . . . well, other things!!! Remember, there is nothing sexier than a sense of humor. And, laughter and variety are the keys to a great sex life.

Happy Valentine's Day, you crazy kids!

pretty fun tip: Keep it sensual! To create a more romantic setting, think about using all your senses, especially smell. Go for flowers that have a pretty scent, like roses, lilacs, lilies, peonies, gardenia, freesia, and jasmine. I also love using scented oils on my body. I personally like them better than perfume, because they soak into the skin and blend with your own natural smell. Look for one that has notes with aphrodisiac properties, like vanilla, amber, tuberose, jasmine, ylang-ylang, night jasmine, sandalwood, or neroli.

whipped two ways

Mexican hot chocolate and rose-flavored whipped creams add a little spiced-up romance to any classic breakfast staple (cinnamon and rose are both natural aphrodisiacs). Use these whips to show some extra love, whether you're making French toast, pancakes, or waffles—and yes, you have permission to make them from a mix.

Use these whips to show some extra love.

MEXICAN HOT CHOCOLATE WHIP

MAKES ABOUT 2 CUPS

1 tablespoon unsweetened
  cocoa powder
4 teaspoons sugar
1 teaspoon cinnamon
¼ teaspoon cayenne pepper
1 cup heavy cream

Place the bowl of a stand mixer and the whisk attachment, or a large metal bowl and whisk, in the freezer for 10 to 15 minutes.

Combine the cocoa powder, sugar, cinnamon, and cayenne in the bowl. Pour in the cream and stir with a spatula or spoon to combine. Whisk the mixture until the cream gets thick and fluffy and can hold stiff peaks, 1 to 2 minutes. Serve right away or store the whipped cream in an airtight container in the fridge overnight. Whip for another 10 to 15 seconds before serving.

ROSE WHIP

MAKES ABOUT 2 CUPS

1 cup heavy cream
1½ teaspoons sugar
½ teaspoon rose water
Red or pink all-natural
  food coloring

Place the bowl of a stand mixer and the whisk attachment, or a large metal bowl and whisk, in the freezer for 10 to 15 minutes.

Combine the cream, sugar, and rose water in the bowl. Add 2 to 3 small drops of food coloring, then whisk until the cream gets thick and fluffy and can hold stiff peaks, 1 to 2 minutes. Serve right away or store the whipped cream in an airtight container in the fridge overnight. Whip for another 10 to 15 seconds before serving.

Cozy Pop-Up Party

One of the most special things about having a tribe of friends who feel like family is that there's rarely an inconvenient time for them to come over, and when they do—no matter what we get up to—it feels welcome and grounding. I love that the most cherished people in my life feel comfortable enough to show up unannounced, and know that by the time I finish putting the kids to bed, we can have the kind of connective, recharging night that comes from spending time with the people who know you best. And when you have the kind of home that everyone feels warm and welcome in, suddenly you find yourself hosting a lot more pop-up parties, whether it's an evening of deep, substantive conversation or simply your friends crashing your solo viewing party of *The Bachelor*. There's no need to scramble to clean up or make anything look too nice—just dim the lights, grab all the blankets and pillows you have, and make a big loungy pit. Pull together something to eat from your Pretty Stocked Pantry (page 200) or whip up a batch of Chilaquiles (page 89)—my all-time favorite breakfast-for-dinner recipe. Open a bottle of wine, or better yet, make a pitcher of Ginger-Thyme Margaritas (page 92). Then take a moment to express gratitude for these incredible, smart, strong, funny individuals and the fact that you get to close the chapter of this day in their company.

chilaquiles two ways

Everybody loves chilaquiles. I mean, eggs served over crispy tortillas that have been braised in a spiced sauce and sprinkled with queso fresco, crisp radishes, and plenty of fresh cilantro? And maybe even some sour cream, avocado, and hot sauce? Yes, please. What I love about this dish is that you can do it to suit your mood and timetable. You can use green or red versions of the sauce, in case you love one more than the other (I'm a tomatillo kind of girl), and you can make your own tortilla chips in the oven or buy a bag at the store and call it a day. You could even buy a rotisserie chicken and add the shredded meat (or use leftovers from Roasted Chicken, (page 236), if you want to make this even heartier. And while fried eggs taste the best—and flipping them in the pan is a great party trick (which I'm pretty good at, if you ask me)—you can scramble a big batch if you don't feel like making them to order. And if you want to keep things light, just use egg whites.

Preheat the oven to 400°F.

Cut the tortillas into chip-sized triangles, about 8 per tortilla. Lightly coat 2 large baking sheets with the oil—or line it with parchment if you want even easier cleanup—and scatter the chips on the sheet. Drizzle them with a bit more oil, sprinkle with a pinch of salt, and toss to coat. Arrange the chips so they're in a single layer and don't overlap.

Bake the chips for 10 to 12 minutes, flipping them halfway through and watching to make sure they don't burn. They should be golden brown and crisp. Remove the chips and set aside. Keep the oven on and decrease the heat to 350°F.

Combine the chips in a large sided sheet pan or a cast-iron skillet. Pour the salsa or enchilada sauce plus tomatoes over the top and give everything a toss so the

SERVES 6 TO 8

8 6-inch whole wheat or corn tortillas
Extra virgin olive oil
Kosher salt, to taste
3½ cups store-bought green tomatillo salsa (for green) or 2½ cups store-bought enchilada sauce plus 1 cup canned diced tomatoes (for red)
2 to 3 cups shredded chicken (optional)
1 cup shredded queso fresco
Unsalted butter, for cooking the eggs (optional)

chilaquiles two ways (continued)

chips are well coated. Spread the chicken over the top and sprinkle with the cheese. Bake for 10 to 15 minutes, until the sauce is warmed through and the cheese is nice and melty. Feel free to finish under the broiler for about 20 seconds to get the cheese browned and bubbly.

Meanwhile, make the eggs: If frying the eggs, add the butter or 1 tablespoon olive oil to a large nonstick or cast-iron skillet over medium heat. Gently crack two eggs into the skillet with plenty of room between them. Cook until the bottoms are set and the edges golden, 1 to 2 minutes. Carefully slide a spatula under each egg and flip (or go for glory and flip the eggs with a flick of the wrist—maybe check out some videos on YouTube before performing for company!). Cook for about 1 minute, until the whites have set but the yolks are still runny. Transfer the eggs to individual plates and repeat with the remaining eggs.

If scrambling the eggs, whisk them in a bowl and season with a pinch of salt and pepper. Add 1 tablespoon olive oil to a large nonstick or cast-iron skillet over high heat. When the oil begins to shimmer, pour the eggs into the pan and slowly stir with a spatula. When the eggs begin to set (it will look like curds forming), reduce the heat to low and continue stirring until the eggs are just set and fluffy, about 2 minutes.

To serve, remove the pan from the oven and top each fried egg with a good scoop of sauce, a sprinkle of cilantro and cheese, a dollop of sour cream, and a few slices of radish and avocado. For scrambled eggs, top the sauce with the eggs and pretty it up with the sliced avocado and radishes, plus a sprinkle of cilantro. Serve with lime wedges and hot sauce.

6 to 8 large eggs (1 per person)
½ cup sliced radishes, for serving
1 avocado, sliced, for serving
2 tablespoons chopped fresh cilantro, for serving
1 lime cut into wedges, for serving
Sour cream, for serving
Hot sauce, for serving

Do It Light

I know it can be fun to put out a big junket convenience store buffet when you're pulling together a party on the fly, but consider these slightly healthier options for mindless munching:

* Amp up air-popped popcorn by tossing it with curry powder, garlic powder, or chopped fresh herbs plus a little olive or coconut oil.

* Drain a can of chickpeas, pat them dry, and toss with just enough olive oil to coat, plus a sprinkle of cumin, cayenne, and salt. Spread on a baking sheet and bake in the oven at 400°F for 30 minutes!

* Pair store-bought root vegetable chips with a super-quick dip. Mix a low-fat Greek yogurt with prepared horseradish and add lemon zest, salt, and pepper.

* Create an exotic combo of dried fruit (cherries, figs, apricots, mangoes) for a dried fruit salad. Add some mixed nuts or seeds and carob chips, for trail mix!

* When in doubt, keep it classic: fresh fruit and veggie sticks with hummus are always delicious and so easy!

Other ideas for cozy pop-up parties:

With close friends and good company, pretty much anything can become a reason for a stay-warm-inside gathering:

* Knitting circle
* Planning give-back initiatives in your community like sponsoring a family of refugees
* Movie marathon
* Meditation or restorative yoga
* First fireplace fire-up, complete with s'mores and weenies
* First snow
* Learn something new—how to read the tarot or playing mah jongg

ginger-thyme margaritas

This is a Do It Light recipe in disguise as a cocktail, because the ingredients all have healing properties that are extra handy throughout the winter: Ginger is a powerful anti-inflammatory, thyme can do everything from soothe the belly to ward off coughs and colds, and tequila—yes, tequila!—can help you get a better night's sleep and won't leave you feeling hung over (assuming it's 100 percent agave). I'm not suggesting that you down three or four margaritas in the name of medicine, but if you're going to have a drink, go with one that's a good, clean buzz. In fact, many of the cocktail recipes in this book are tequila libations for this very reason.

In a small saucepot, combine the honey, ginger, and thyme with 1 cup water. Bring to a boil, reduce to a simmer and heat for 5 minutes. Turn off the heat and let the pot sit uncovered for 30 minutes so the flavors meld. Strain the simple syrup into a jar and store in the refrigerator until ready to use.

In a large pitcher, combine the tequila, lime juice, and ½ cup simple syrup. Stir and adjust to taste, with more simple syrup or lime juice as desired.

To serve, salt the rim of your margarita glasses by running a lime around the edge and dipping the glass into the salt. Fill the glasses with ice, pour in the margarita mix, and top with a splash of sparkling water. Garnish with a sprig of fresh thyme.

MAKES 6 COCKTAILS

1 cup honey

4 tablespoons fresh ginger, chopped

2 bunches fresh thyme, plus more for garnish

1½ cups 100 percent agave tequila

1¼ cups fresh-squeezed lime juice (about 10 to 12 limes)

1 lime, cut into wedges, to serve

Kosher salt, to serve

Ice

San Pellegrino or other sparkling water

Family Dinner Night: Happy Hump Day

We have always been a family that recognizes the importance of a home-cooked meal.

My mom's mom, the daughter of two Hungarian Jewish immigrants, made the most delicious food, Jewish-American classics like matzo ball soup and brisket were her specialties. My mom, whose dad was from the South, took that to another level by marrying these two cooking traditions and coming up with the ultimate comfort food repertoire. Plus, as the greatest one-pot cook of all time, she's the queen of taking whatever's hanging out in the fridge and making something crazy delicious.

You can make an otherwise ordinary family meal even more special by adding touches that are meaningful to your heritage. If you don't already know about them, ask your parents or grandparents about your family's history and any traditions there might have been before your time. Even if there aren't heirloom recipes that have been passed down for generations, see if you can find a dish or two that comes from that part of the world. It's not only a great topic of conversation, but it's also extremely grounding for your children—and you—to know where your roots are.

mom's beef stroganoff

My mom—or Gogo, as the boys call her—perfected this recipe, and it's now a classic in our family. It's all about using the best-quality sirloin and good, fresh mushrooms, and seasoning simply with just salt and pepper. Heaped on a bed of egg noodles with a little dollop of sour cream? It doesn't get more comforting, or more perfect for sharing on a cold winter night, than that. I've added a pinch of paprika to the mix for a little heat and to add a taste of Hungary to an otherwise traditional Russian dish.

Serve this dish with roasted veggies like broccoli or cauliflower. It's easy and doesn't take a long time to cook—just toss the florets with olive oil and salt, then pop in the oven at 425°F for 20 minutes or until just browned. Add a loaf of good, warm bread and butter and call it dinner.

SERVES 6

¼ cup unsalted butter

½ yellow onion, finely chopped

2 garlic cloves, minced

1 pound sirloin steak, cut into 1-inch cubes

Kosher salt, to taste

Freshly ground black pepper, to taste

8 ounces cremini or white button mushrooms, stems trimmed and thinly sliced

1 cup plus 3 tablespoons beef stock

3 tablespoons almond flour

¼ cup sour cream

1 teaspoon paprika

One 12-ounce bag egg noodles, cooked according to package instructions

Heat the butter in a large skillet over medium-high heat. When it begins to foam, add the onions and garlic to the pan and cook until just translucent, 2 minutes. Season the steak with salt and pepper and add the meat to the pan. Cook for about 6 minutes or until browned on all sides. Add the mushrooms and 1 cup of beef stock with a pinch of salt and let that get all juicy—until the mushrooms are tender—about 4 minutes.

In a small pan over medium heat, bring the remaining 3 tablespoons of stock to a simmer. Add the almond flour and whisk until combined. Cook for a minute or two, just to remove any flour flavor. Scoop the roux into the pan with the meat and mushrooms. Bring the pan to a boil while stirring in the roux. Let the mixture boil until it thickens, 1 to 2 minutes.

Remove the pan from the heat and stir in the sour cream and paprika. Adjust the seasoning if necessary and serve over the egg noodles.

WHAT'S YOUR TABLESCAPE STYLE?

As you can probably tell by now, I'm definitely a boho kind of girl. But what's right for free-spirit me might not be your midcentury tumbler of iced tea. Just as you determine how you like to decorate your living space over time—clean Scandinavian minimalist versus farmhouse eclectic, or all-white everything versus big, bold colors—the same goes for your table, or "tablescape." From the linens, glassware, dishware, and silverware to the serving dishes and centerpieces, your tablescape should be a reflection of you and what you find lovely and beautiful (an instant vibe booster). Once you define your go-to style, it gets easier to make décor choices for each party you throw, since you have your foundational pieces and just need to layer on touches that refine your party's visual concept and feel. Remember that there's nothing written in stone when it comes to defining your aesthetic. Even the most minimalist gal can soften things up with floral touches once in a while, or just because you're into a Mad Hatter's tea party kind of feel doesn't mean you can't streamline with simple linens or more modern glassware for certain occasions. Once you've put your finger on what exactly it is that you like, then you can keep an eye out for new pieces to add to your collection. Here are a few timeless design categories to help you curate your own tablescape style.

MODERN MINIMALIST

SIGNATURES: Clean and symmetrical lines; geometric shapes (but more squares than circles); mostly white and black with bold accent colors (or white on white on white); glass and metal; natural fabrics like silks and cotton. Less is more. Simple and polished, but not stuffy.

STARTER PIECES: A crisp white tablecloth (cotton or linen), thin-stemmed silverware, unadorned white ceramic serving trays, Marimekko or IKEA anything.

BOHEMIAN ECLECTIC

SIGNATURES: Mix-and-match patterns and textures; free and flowy fabrics; global influence; warmer materials like pewter and ceramics; earthy touches like feathers, antlers, and mosses; unconventional uses for found objects, especially flea market treasures like antique birdcages, old-school toolboxes, soda crates, biscuit tins, canning jars, and bottles (all perfect for displaying food, candles, or flowers). Laid-back, quirky, and fun.

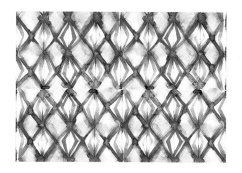

STARTER PIECES: An ikat or shibori tablecloth, driftwood cutting boards, hand-thrown serving bowls, sheepskin and/or jewel-toned seat cushions.

SHABBY CHIC/PROVENÇAL

SIGNATURES: Softer colors like pastels and antique whites; floral patterns; mismatched silverware and plates in a coordinating color palette; vintage serving pieces. A little rumpled, broken in, and casual. Sweet, but not *too* sweet.

STARTER PIECES: A vintage floral tablecloth (cotton or linen), a flea market silverware set, cut glass goblets or tumblers, barn wood serving trays.

MIDNIGHT GLAM

SIGNATURES: Traditional lines but with the colors and textures turned *way* up: rich, dark colors like golds, blacks, and reds; damask fabrics; high candles (a candelabra would not be out of place on this table). Floor-length tablecloths; ornate shapes and extra frills, especially in serving pieces, are a plus. Formal, sexy, and dramatic.

STARTER PIECES: A black damask tablecloth, chalice-style wineglasses, black milk glass chargers, a pewter or bronze candelabra.

TABLESCAPE BASICS

Once you get an idea of your tablescape style, you can start building your own collection of treasures that you reach for whenever you entertain. By keeping a stash of table décor essentials, you can dress a table up or down to suit your style, mood, or occasion. Don't be afraid to mix high with low, clean with a little bit funky. Stores like Crate & Barrel, Pottery Barn, and Williams-Sonoma offer tried-and-true basics, which you can offset with flea market, estate sale, or vintage show finds or quirky touches from online stores like Etsy. And always keep an eye out for new and interesting things when you're traveling. I especially love bringing back unique textiles that reflect where in the world they're from. If there are really decadent pieces you're loving but don't have the budget for, give yourself permission to collect over time. My mom has the most beautiful set of china for which she's been gathering pieces for years, and I've added to it on special occasions. Let your partner, family, friends, etc., know that for your birthday you'd love that beautiful gravy boat or pitcher. You'll pay them back with beautiful parties!

These are a few of my favorite elements to play with when I'm setting a table.

* **SIMPLE WHITE PLATES:** These are the little black dress for the table. They always look polished and handsome and complement any decoration. Plus, food looks so much more appetizing on white than on any other color.

* **MODERN DRINKING GLASSES:** A versatile glass with clean lines (meaning clear glass and no ornamentation) is the simple white plate equivalent for glassware. They go with everything.

* **CHARGERS:** These large flat dishes are a great investment because you can completely and quickly change the vibe of a table with them. Go wicker, color-blocked, or pewter—or get your Liberace on and go all gold and frilly and Swarovski-crystallized.

* **TEXTILES:** Things like tablecloths, cloth napkins, and place mats lend texture and personality to the table, from whimsical and sweet to luxurious and plush. Definitely think outside the box on this one—a piece of great fabric can easily double as a tablecloth, and place mats can be made from cut-down woven textiles like flat-weave rugs or even vintage prints.

* **SILVERWARE:** Whether you're keeping things unadorned and modern or super-ornate and feminine, just pick something that feels good in your hand. If you're on a budget, comb flea markets to assemble a mismatched set—and serving pieces too!—which can easily be polished up to look almost like new (just do a quick online search for how to do it). It's a sweet touch, no matter what your tablescape style is.

* **PLATTERS AND SERVING DISHES:** These are the pieces to collect over time. I love how my bowls, platters, and trays have a story to tell, whether it was a treasure I found while traveling, stumbled across while checking out a local artist's workshop, or was given as a gift. If you're just starting to assemble your tableware stockpile, look for simple, versatile pieces that can be used in many ways: wooden cutting boards can double as trays or trivets, classic white bowls or platters look chic on any spread, rustic wooden salad bowls and platters add

warmth yet still look fantastic on even the most minimalist table, and sturdy enameled pots and baking dishes always look great going from oven to table.

CENTERPIECES

Adding a lovely touch to the middle of the table is so simple to do and goes a really long way in tying together your table-scape and party theme, while also drawing in guests and making them feel welcome. Here are a few ideas.

* **FLOWERS:** The classic choice, and the quickest way to add life to a table. Start by thinking about your colors, then see what options your local florist, farmers' market, or grocery store have. Consider what feels right for your table or your party's theme—elegant lilies have a different vibe from a spray of hydrangea, and lush bundles of peonies feel different on a table from bud vases with wisps of lavender (yes, herbs can be used in arrangements too!). Even something as simple as fern fronds can look great in an interesting vase. Just remember to keep arrangements low enough so they won't block anyone's line of sight.

* **CANDLES:** I love the warmth that candles bring to a table. The sky's the limit in terms of how creative you can get; just scale it to your table. Tea lights feel daintier than pillar candles in large glass hur-

ricanes, for example. See what suits the occasion and mood, as well as the style you're going for. Tall tapers in a candelabra or pillars sitting on ornate pedestals can add drama, while candles set in canning jars lend a more homey vibe.

* **SOMETHING NATURAL:** One of my favorite ways to add texture and interest to a table is bringing the outdoors in. Rocks, feathers, seashells or sea glass, beautiful leaves, moss, herbs from the garden—just about anything can look beautiful if you coordinate it with the colors on the table and arrange it in interesting ways.

* **SOMETHING OLD:** Apothecary bottles, vintage trays, or even found objects (like the aforementioned antique birdcage, toolbox, or biscuit tin) can add to the personality and warmth of your tablescape, plus they're great conversation starters.

* **A LITTLE SOMETHING SWEET:** Candy as a centerpiece is fun, especially when you color-coordinate it with the table and theme. Nowadays you can find candy in just about every color imaginable, and it looks super-polished when you pick a few shades of the same color and sort them into individual glass containers. Or if you're feeling ambitious, create an ombré effect. You can also consider on-theme options like old-school candies, candies that look like sporting equipment, etc. Just add a few glass dishes or jars, and you're in business.

SPRING

Mom's Favorite Things Brunch

To me, Mother's Day is one of the most important holidays of the year. It's when we come together to honor the women who gave us life, who raised us to be the people we are, who taught us the lessons we'll always carry in our hearts, and who both ground us and lift us up with their support. Now that I'm a mother myself, I'm so humbled by this day, because I've started to see the circle of life—all of us kids growing up and becoming parents, our family tree sprouting more and more branches. When you take a moment to reflect on that—giving thanks for all the gifts in your life from your mother, and maybe also receiving the thanks that others are passing on to you—this day becomes a pretty powerful one.

My celebration usually starts with the kids bringing me breakfast in bed. Ryder and Bing always *both* want to make me a cappuccino, because they know how much I love them, so I get two! Then the entire family gets together for brunch in honor of us mothers: my mom, my sister-in-law, my aunt Patty, my cousin Joey. The kids and husbands are in charge of planning everything, though somehow we always end up having to lend a hand (every mom reading this is probably nodding in agreement right now!). But it's special and sweet, and we're always so grateful that we can all hit pause in our busy lives to spend the day together.

To start planning your own celebration of all things Mom, think about your mother's favorite things: What's her signature color? Does she love a certain animal? Does she collect anything? What's her birthstone? What's her favorite flower? Any guilty pleasures? Use the answers to come up with your theme and color scheme. If there's a trip she's always wanted to take but hasn't been able to, bring it to her! Take her to the beach with a tropical fruit spread, bright sprays of hibiscus, and playful ukulele music; or add a taste of Paris with cinnamon-sugar crepes, macaroons, and berets for everyone. The more tailored it is to Mom, the more genuine your celebration of her will feel. Think of it as a living, breathing thank-you note to her.

Do It Right

HOW TO BUILD A BRUNCH

To me, there's only one way to brunch—with *all* the classics!

Eggs + Sausage/Bacon + Potatoes +
Waffles/French Toast/Crepes + Bagels
(with Cream Cheese, Sliced Veggies, Lox, and Whitefish/Tuna Salad)

Of course, not every component needs to be on the table, so pick which ones you and your family love most, and then add touches that reinforce your theme. Maybe it's a dish or two that represent different chapters of your mom's life, like where her family is from, places she's traveled, where she met your dad, or where she was living when she had you. Maybe there are traditional dishes that no family gathering would be complete without. Or maybe it's just something she really, really loves to eat! Finish off the table with fresh fruit and juice, coffee, and a selection of teas (for tips, see Tea-Tasting Garden Party on page 131).

Do It Light

Below are my favorite healthy versions of brunch staples. I especially love that they're really just a canvas. You can add just about anything to a frittata, and the latkes can just as easily be made with regular potatoes, sweet potatoes, or winter squash.

Other great frittata combos:

* Caramelized onions, blue cheese, and plenty of black pepper

* Roasted squash, goat cheese, and sage

* Sun-dried tomatoes, olives, and feta

* Roasted pepper, arugula, and pancetta

* Fresh herbs and ricotta

* Wild mushrooms, leek, and fontina

frittata with asparagus, sweet peas, and prosciutto

This is fresh, light, and perfect for spring. Serve it as a part of brunch or as an easy lunch with some greens and a cold rosé.

Preheat the oven to 375°F.

In a large bowl, beat the eggs with 2 tablespoons water and season with the salt and pepper. Stir in the cheese and prosciutto.

In a large ovenproof skillet, heat the olive oil over medium heat. Add the onion and cook, stirring, until just translucent, about 2 minutes. Add the asparagus and peas, season with salt and pepper, and cook, stirring, until tender but not browned, 4 to 5 minutes.

Stir the egg mixture so the cheese and prosciutto aren't settled at the bottom of the bowl and pour into the skillet. Stir to evenly distribute all the ingredients. Cook until the bottom is just set, about 3 minutes. Carefully lift the edges of the frittata to allow the uncooked eggs to seep underneath. Transfer the pan to the oven and cook for about 10 minutes, or until the center is nearly set.

Preheat the broiler. Broil the frittata for about 1 minute, until the top is just beginning to brown. Either place the skillet directly on your brunch spread (a nice, homey touch if it's in a cast-iron skillet) or loosen the edges of the frittata with a knife or spatula so that you can carefully flip it onto a large plate. Slice and serve warm or at room temperature.

SERVES 10

1 dozen large eggs

½ teaspoon kosher salt, plus more to taste

½ teaspoon freshly ground black pepper, plus more to taste

1 cup shredded Gruyère, packed

4 ounces thinly sliced prosciutto, chopped

2 tablespoons extra virgin olive oil

1 small yellow onion, diced

1 bunch asparagus, woody ends trimmed and cut into ¼-inch pieces (about 1 cup)

1 cup fresh or frozen sweet pea

baked zucchini and spring onion latkes

Traditional latkes gets a makeover with fresh market veggies and no frying required.

Preheat the oven to 425°F. Line two large sided baking sheets with parchment paper.

In a food processor or with a large box grater, grate the zucchini, potato, and onions. Transfer the mixture to a salad spinner and spin until no more liquid drains (you might want to do this a few times, just to be sure). If you don't have a salad spinner, you can place the mixture in a clean dishtowel or cheesecloth (work in batches), gather up the sides, and squeeze out as much moisture as you can. In a large bowl, combine the zucchini mixture with the rest of the ingredients. Mix well.

Coat the baking sheets lightly with olive oil, then use a 1/4-cup measuring cup to drop the latke mixture on the baking sheet, flattening each to about 1/4 inch thick.

Bake for 20 minutes, flip, and bake 20 minutes more, or until the latkes are cooked through and crispy around the edges. Serve them piled high on a plate or platter.

MAKES 15 TO 20

2 medium zucchini

1 medium Yukon Gold potato

2 spring onions or 1 small white onion

2 eggs, lightly beaten

1 tablespoon extra virgin olive oil, plus more for the baking sheet

1 cup almond flour

1½ teaspoons kosher salt

½ teaspoon freshly ground black pepper

Do It Easy

MIMOSA AND BELLINI BAR

A really classy touch that's beyond simple to pull off is a Mimosa and Bellini Bar. Set out champagne, cava, or prosecco with a variety of juices and fruit purees (berry, melon, orange, grapefruit, pineapple, peach, pomegranate). For extra credit, put together cute cups of sliced fruit to go with each option you serve as pretty garnishes. Be sure to include sparkling water for anyone who might just want a spritzer, and keep everything on ice.

Easter/Spring Celebration

Easter is a standout holiday in our house. It's just one of those holidays that our family has always made a point of going all in for, which makes the tradition that much more meaningful and definitely something we all look forward to. Plus, I love that the day has roots in rebirth and renewal—for the grass and trees and flowers coming back into full bloom, and for all of us coming out of our winter hibernation to gather once again. Perhaps it doesn't have any religious significance for you, but you certainly do not need to attach any to this celebration to make it beautiful. Call it spring! Call it the vernal equinox! Some people go to church, but for me Easter is all about the kids and candy (a special once-in-a-while treat) and having fun on a beautiful day. We'll dye eggs together the night before so we're not making a big mess the day of the party, and they usually end up crazy looking and covered in glitter, perfectly imperfect and awesome. For décor, I keep things fairly traditional: flowers, plus pretty touches like old birdcages, which I hang from the trees or use as centerpieces, and fill with moss and little eggs. Or I'll go totally rogue and change things up completely, like the year I did a Jamaican-themed Easter, complete with jerk chicken, plantains, rice and beans, and beef patties. There's no right way to "Easter" in my opinion!

Whatever route you go, it all comes down to getting the kids outside and celebrating spring, complete with eggs, carrots, and bunnies galore. That's also what I'm thinking about when I set my menu, so I usually riff on things like deviled eggs with untraditional fillings (think pesto, wasabi, curry, or even miso) or dips that I pair with baby carrots with their green tops still attached. Another current favorite of mine and the kids' is Carrot-Date "Shakes" (they're really just smoothies that are loaded with healthy ingredients).

Do It Easy

COOKIE CRAFT

When it's time to take a break from the sun—or if you're in need of a rainy-day option—set kids up with this super-easy activity. All you need are store-bought or homemade plain sugar cookies (ideally shaped like Easter-themed items) and lots of different decorating options, like icing or frosting, sanding sugars, sprinkles, sugar flowers, sugar pearls, and edible confetti and glitter. Make it part of your tablescape by creating individual stations: Set each place with a small, rimmed baking sheet (the disposable aluminum versions you can buy at the grocery store are great for this). Set two or three cookies on each sheet, along with ramekins or small cups filled with each topping. The finished product can also do double duty as a favor if you send kids home with their creations in cellophane bags tied up with twine or ribbon.

carrot-date "shakes"

These faux shakes are just as creamy as the real thing, plus they're loaded with the good-for-you stuff (carrots, sweet potatoes, super-powered chia seeds) and sweetened lightly and naturally with dates and maple syrup, honey, or agave. It's a great way to get some veggies into the kids before they stuff themselves with sugar. They look supercute served in little glasses with decorative straws, and the orange color is a pretty addition to your Easter table. You *could* also make an adult version by adding a splash of bourbon.

MAKES TEN 6-OUNCE SMOOTHIES

2 cups shredded carrot (about 2 carrots), frozen

2 cups shredded sweet potato (about 1 small potato), frozen

2 medium bananas, frozen

8 dates, pitted and soaked in warm water for 10 minutes

1 vanilla bean, seeds scraped

1 teaspoon cinnamon

½ teaspoon nutmeg

One 13.5-ounce can coconut milk

2 cups unsweetened nut milk or water

2 tablespoons maple syrup, agave, or honey (optional)

In a blender, combine all the ingredients and sweetener, if using. Blend until completely smooth. Adjust the consistency with water if necessary—it should be a little thinner than a milkshake. Taste and adjust the sweetness to your liking.

pretty fun tip: Make sure to freeze the grated carrots and sweet potatoes before blending; it'll make the texture of the shakes even smoother and creamier.

Bestie's Bachelorette

Spring and summer are peak wedding season, which is why I've included this time-honored tradition here. We've all witnessed that moment when a bachelorette party comes rolling into a bar with the penis hats, penis beads, penis sashes—penis, penis, penis—and things get a little out of hand. Well, you're about to be that girl. Hosting a bachelorette can really just be an excuse to drink a little (or a lot) too much and share funny (see also: embarrassing) stories about the bride-to-be. But it's also a time when you and your girls get to do it up as a tribe and send off one of your own into the next chapter of her life. The goal is to strike the perfect balance that's a little bit classy and just the right amount of trashy.

Since most bachelorette parties end up at the bar/strip club/casino, consider your get-together the pre-party, or what you're going to do from about 7 P.M. until 10 P.M., when you decide it is time to move on to your next destination. The worst thing that could happen: You are having so much fun that you decide to stay home. But something tells me it's going to be one epic night. Buckle up; things are about to get pretty rowdy.

Bachelorette do's and don'ts:

✳ **Do** tap in to your tribe. Get on the phone with your girlfriends, get organized, and divvy up responsibilities. Who is going to do the food? Drinks? Fun favors? Is there going to be any "entertainment"? How naughty do you want the whole affair to be? Is the bride a bit prudish, or will she spill all her secrets?

✳ **Do** think about how to put the bride-to-be *slightly* out of her comfort zone. Is she always put together just so? Find her a crazy outfit to wear, tease her hair, and give her an eighties glam makeover. Does she love to sing but would never, ever do it in front of anyone? Karaoke!

✳ **Do** assign your guests something to bring that represents who the bride-to-be was before she met her partner: a trinket, memory, story, or photo from her single days. Then, sit in a circle together and share the story of why you chose that particular object—the more detailed the better. Remember, the goal is to create conversation and get the laughter going.

✳ **Do** serve her favorite drink from high school/college/happy hour, whether it's Mike's Hard Lemonade, Boone's Farm, Zima, or dirty martinis. Other than that: *full bar*. And definitely *do* look online for fun bachelorette-themed drinking games.

✳ **Do** have snacks on hand. There's no bigger recipe for disaster than drinking on an empty stomach. I steer clear of anything too heavy that will leave people feeling sleepy and instead put out a selection of light, no-cook munchies, like veggies and spreads, pesto-topped crostini, chips with a variety of salsas, pretzels, and popcorn. Feel free to infuse the spirit of the night into your spread: breadsticks with bocconcini, baby carrots and cherry tomatoes, salami sticks with black olives . . . you get the idea.

✱ **Don't** be afraid of a theme and dressing up (pinup girls, country cute, brothel madams, wearing your old bridesmaid dresses . . .).

✱ **Don't** cross the line where you're compromising the bride-to-be's ethics or boundaries.

✱ **Don't** be above wearing matching personalized items, like T-shirts, temporary tattoos, tank tops, hats, etc.

✱ **Don't** hesitate to make it a slumber party, complete with matching bathrobes and late-night snacks.

✱ **Don't** think that you can't do all these things with your friends on a regular Saturday night.

is that a banana in your pants? pops

There's nothing restrained about a bachelorette party, so the food shouldn't be either. But this dessert perfectly combines clean eating and dirty minds. Serve with a round of coffee shots before you call the taxis for part two of the epic party night.

MAKES 10 SERVINGS

5 ripe but firm bananas

10 Popsicle sticks

One 12-ounce bag dark chocolate, chopped, or semisweet chocolate chips

2 tablespoons vegetable oil

Almonds or walnuts, crushed (optional)

Dehydrated strawberries, raspberries, or pomegranate, finely crumbled (optional)

Shredded unsweetened coconut (optional)

Sea salt (optional)

Line a large baking sheet with foil or parchment paper.

Cut the bananas in half and insert a Popsicle stick into the sliced end. Arrange the bananas on the baking sheet and freeze for 15 minutes.

Combine the chocolate with the oil and melt, either in the microwave on low or in the top of a double boiler (or in a heat-proof bowl set on top of a small pot of simmering water). Stir until smooth.

Dip the bananas into the chocolate until fully coated. Before the chocolate sets, sprinkle with the decorative toppings of your choice. Place the bananas back on the baking sheet and freeze until the chocolate sets, about 30 minutes. Arrange on a pretty tray and serve immediately, or store in the freezer in an airtight container for up to a week.

FAVOR BAG:
OH-SHIT KIT

Thank all your guests—and help them out with the morning after—with an assortment of hangover cures: Advil, Emergen-C, a little face mist, a bottle of water, under-eye cream, Pepto-Bismol, a small bottle of coconut water, protein bars, and mints. To make it meaningful, include a small, personalized gift that says, "I survived Bachelorette [insert the bride's future last name]."

Tea-Tasting Garden Party

Tasting parties are such a fun way to change up the usual dinner party, luncheon, or brunch. Invite a handful of friends—between six and twelve is the magic number, enough to have good mingling and conversation, not so many that it will be difficult to compare tasting notes—and put out a spread for everyone to sample, whether it's beer, wine, cheese, honey, oil, apples, etc. Then have everyone share their thoughts. These events are a great way to not only learn a lot about a certain food or drink type, but they also spark great connection among your guests. I especially love the idea of a tea tasting because it's a Do It Light option that is also the perfect excuse to throw a charming garden party. But you can use the same setup for any kind of tasting.

Here's how to do it.

TEA-TASTING PARTY 101

✻ **Choose your teas:** Shoot for four to eight teas—you want enough so that you have an interesting variety, but not so many that people lose track of what they tasted. I recommend visiting a specialty tea shop and enlisting the help of someone to put together a good assortment since there are *tons* of different kinds of tea: greens, whites, oolongs, Earl Greys, herbals.

Pick what speaks to you. Also have them guide you in terms of how much tea to buy and how to prepare each tea. Since it will most likely be warm outside, see if there are any varieties that are nice when served iced. Figure that each guest is going to have about a half cup of each.

✳ **Pretty up the presentation:** If you're going for a proper English setup, find decorative teapots to hold the teas. Or if you're feeling a Zen garden vibe, look for little ceramic bowls. Make a label for each tea so guests know which is which, along with a few notes, like where the tea comes from, historical tidbits, health properties, or fun facts. Since dry tea leaves can also be beautiful, you can put out little dishes of unprepared tea for guests to see and smell. Also set out pens and paper for everyone to take notes as they taste.

✳ **Break it down for guests:** Once everyone has poured their first cup, grabbed a plate of food, and settled in, make a toast welcoming everyone (remember Party Rule #4!) and explain how the tasting will work. Keep it casual—there won't be a test!—but do encourage everyone to taste, take notes, compare notes, and rank the teas. Announce the "winner" when everyone has finished working through the selections. Here's a few commonly used tea-tasting terms to get your guests going, but consider asking your local expert to add his or her two cents.

TEA LINGO CHEAT SHEET

Flavor descriptors:

- ✳ Bright
- ✳ Citrusy

- ✳ Flowery
- ✳ Fruity

- ✳ Malty
- ✳ Smoky

Other characteristics:

- ✳ Astringent
- ✳ Balanced
- ✳ Complex

- ✳ Flat
- ✳ Full-bodied
- ✳ Pungent

- ✳ Smooth
- ✳ Strong/weak

SAY A LITTLE SOMETHING: THE RITUAL OF TEA

In addition to explaining how the tasting works and thanking guests for coming, a nice touch for this party would be describing the significance of a tea ritual. Tea ceremonies are a part of a number of cultures in places as diverse as China, Japan, Korea, Britain, Morocco, Russia, and India. The teas and rituals are different, but what they have in common is that the acts of making and enjoying tea are sacred. The ritual offers a brief moment to pause and reflect, as well as connect—whether we're enjoying the tea alone and thinking about our day and intentions for what remains of it, or we're sharing it with others and taking time to appreciate one another's company. I love how a cup of tea can be quiet and meditative, enjoyed while journaling or just looking out the window, but also communal and social. Allowing your guests to think about the significance of the ritual for them will help add deeper meaning to their tasting experience.

Do It Easy

DIY SALAD BAR IN A JAR

At a tasting party it's important to coordinate the food with whatever it is you're tasting. Olive oil would pair really nicely with a round of simple pizzas, fresh from the oven or grill. Instead of traditional charcuterie for a cheese-tasting party, go for fruit pairings: brie and apples, chèvre and cherries, blue cheese and peaches (especially grilled!), gouda and pears. If you're pairing up beer, see how different types affect the heat level of spicy foods (Indian, Korean, Thai). For tea, the ideal meal is light (so it doesn't overpower the teas) and simple (so it doesn't overpower your energy as a host). For a fresh tea party brunch, set out all the makings for a nice big salad that guests can layer up in a jar and shake (you'll need pint- or quart-sized wide-mouthed jars, at least one for each guest). Here are some ideas for what to include:

- ✳ A variety of lettuces and greens
- ✳ Grains like farro, quinoa, or brown rice
- ✳ Legumes like chickpeas, black beans, or kidney beans
- ✳ Tons of prepped raw veggies—carrots, radishes, jicama, fennel, broccoli, etc.—whatever you love!

* Crunchy bits, like nuts, seeds, toasted pita, or tortilla strips

* Something sweet, like dried cranberries, apricots, or raisins

* Proteins, like chicken, shrimp, hard-boiled eggs, or avocado slices

* A selection of dressings, but be sure to have at least one creamy and one vinaigrette

Do It Light

DRESSING UP

Salad dressings are a fun and easy way to add a homemade touch to an otherwise store-bought meal offering, especially because you can get really creative with new twists on old standbys. This creamy—yet oil-free!—Garden Goddess is a vegan take on a steakhouse classic, while the Turmeric-Citrus Vinaigrette is a light, bright option that's so much more interesting than your usual vinegar–olive oil combo. Plus it packs a nourishing dose of turmeric, which is an ultra-healing superfood that you can find pre-ground in the spice section of just about any grocery store and certainly in health food stores or online.

vegan garden goddess

MAKES ABOUT 2 CUPS

1 ripe avocado

3 large garlic cloves

1 cup fresh basil leaves, packed

3 scallions, whites and greens, roughly chopped

¼ cup fresh lemon juice

1 tablespoon tahini

½ teaspoon crushed red pepper flakes

Salt, to taste

Black pepper, to taste

Combine all the ingredients in a blender with 1 cup water. Blend until smooth. Adjust the consistency with more water if desired and season to taste with salt and pepper. Store in the fridge for up to 4 days.

turmeric-citrus vinaigrette

Combine all the ingredients except the olive oil, salt, and pepper in a blender. Blend until smooth. With the blender running on low speed, very slowly drizzle in the olive oil. Continue blending until the dressing is fully incorporated and smooth. Season to taste with salt and pepper. Store in the fridge for up to 1 week.

MAKES ABOUT 2 CUPS

1 large orange, peeled and roughly chopped

2 garlic cloves

1 tablespoon raw honey

1 tablespoon fresh squeezed lemon juice

4 teaspoons apple cider vinegar

2 teaspoons ground turmeric

1 teaspoon Dijon mustard

⅛ teaspoon cayenne pepper

¾ cup extra virgin olive oil

Kosher salt, to taste

Black pepper, to taste

Everything in this creation is a sign of celebration.

—Ravi Shankar

Just-Add-Rain Pop-Up Party

The tricky thing about entertaining in the spring is that while you want to plan parties outside to take advantage of the newly beautiful weather after winter, there's always the chance of rain spoiling your plans. But this party *insists* on there being some slippery-when-wet fun. Round up your friends at the first sign of a drizzle (assuming there's no lightning in the area); plan some muddy, messy activities for kids and adults to share (flag football! tag! red rover!); and then bring your cookout inside. All you need are trash bags (seriously) and lots of towels.

While this party might look like total mindless fun—which is never a bad thing—there are actually major benefits to getting outside and moving. Personally, I feel completely invigorated by getting some fresh air, rain or shine. All the chatter in my mind quiets down and my body lets go of the tension it's been holding. It's been that way since I was a little girl, and I know I'm not alone. Think back to when you were growing up, the way you'd feel running wild on a summer afternoon: your toes in the grass, your hair still damp from jumping through the sprinklers or swimming in the lake, ocean, or pond. You're not just imagining it—there are proven physiological benefits to getting outside and using your body the way it was meant to be used. Serotonin, a neurotransmitter that helps regulate our mood, increases when we're outside; being in nature reduces stress-related anger and enhances sociability; and all the negative ions native to fresh air have been linked to an improved sense of well-being, heightened awareness and alertness, decreased anxiety, and a lower resting heart rate. Those are all reasons to be extra grateful, even on the gloomiest and wettest of days.

Do It Easy

TRASH BAG SLIP 'N' SLIDE

This is a favorite rainy-day activity in our household. Cut three holes in a large black trash bag—one for your head and two for your arms—then slip on the bag like a poncho. Get a running start on the grass and then slide! If you don't love the idea of hurling yourself full speed across your lawn (though it's seriously fun), you can set up a more traditional slip 'n' slide by laying a plastic painter's drop cloth, tarp, or roll of plastic sheeting on the lawn, then letting 'er rip!

Other ways to have rainy-day fun:

These activities aren't just for kids—feel free to join in too!

* Water balloon fight
* Puddle-splashing contest
* Mud pie bake-off (use leaves, twigs, rocks, or flowers to garnish confections)

- ✳ DIY water park. Add a kiddie pool to the foot of your outdoor play equipment, if you have a slide. Otherwise, it's just one more spot to splash!

- ✳ Just listen. Make sure you carve out some quiet time to just take in the rain and the beautiful sounds it makes.

Do It Right

INDOOR WEENIE ROAST

The only prep required for this fun spread is a quick run to the grocery store. Set out hot dogs and buns with plenty of condiments and toppings (mustard, sriracha, guacamole, chopped onions, pickles, relish, Fritos, shredded cheese). For the grown-ups, serve with Dark and Stormies, perfect for that rainy-day kind of feeling.

dark and stormy two ways

What better to serve on a wet, gloomy day?! Even though these are usually reserved for sunny weather (it's my favorite cooling libation when I'm down in New Orleans), I came up with two variations that are as tasty as the classic but better suited for coming in out of the rain. A Dark and Stormy traditionally consists of dark rum, ginger beer, and lime juice. Since ginger is such a nourishing ingredient (it has natural antibiotic and anti-inflammatory properties) that also gently warms the body, I wanted to showcase it two different ways, hot and cold, with ginger kombucha and ginger tea—plus a splash of rum for good measure. Of course, it bears repeating that these cocktails aren't meant to be *medicine,* but if you're going to be a little naughty, you might as well do it with balance.

DARK AND LIVELY

This version swaps out ginger beer for ginger kombucha, a fermented drink that's packed with good-for-the-gut bacteria. In general, probiotics offer a ton of benefits including improved digestion, mental clarity, and a boosted immune system; and kombucha is one (delicious) form that you can find in most grocery stores and health food shops. To be sure you're buying a product that's authentically good for you—and not just dressed-up juice—look for one that says "naturally fermented" or "never force-carbonated" on the label; is raw (pasteurizing would kill any live bacteria); and contains nothing more than water, tea, sugar, and culture. You need sugar for fermentation, so there will always be some in kombucha, but opt for those that have no more than 3 to 4 grams per serving.

Fill six tall cocktail glasses with ice. Add ¼ cup of the rum to each glass, then top with ½ cup of the kombucha and a squeeze of half a lime. Garnish with the lime wedges.

SERVES 6

Ice
1½ cups dark rum
3 cups ginger kombucha
4 limes, 1 cut into wedges

HOT AND STORMY

This is a sort of mashup between a Dark and Stormy and a hot buttered rum, a spiced warm rum drink with, you guessed it, butter. Instead, I call for ghee, which is a type of clarified butter that's found in Ayurvedic healing traditions. Among many other benefits, it's rich in essential fatty acids, reduces inflammation, and improves digestion. Plus, because it's clarified—meaning it contains no milk solids—it can be tolerated by people who are lactose- or casein-sensitive. You can find it in many grocery stores and health food shops, or online; and put the leftovers to good use by substituting it for olive oil or butter as a cooking fat or just spreading it on toast. For another dose of good-for-you balance, I call for using ginger tea in this recipe instead of hot water.

In a medium heatproof bowl, pour the hot water over the tea bags and let steep for 10 minutes.

In a separate medium bowl, use a rubber spatula to beat together the coconut sugar, ghee, honey, cinnamon, nutmeg, and salt until smooth. Add the rum and steeped tea and stir until the sugar mixture dissolves. Divide among four mugs, garnish each with a cinnamon stick, and serve.

SERVES 4

2 cups boiling water

4 bags ginger tea

$^2/_3$ cup packed coconut sugar

½ cup ghee, room temperature

¼ cup honey

½ teaspoon ground cinnamon

¼ teaspoon ground nutmeg

Pinch of kosher salt

¾ cup dark rum

4 cinnamon sticks, for garnish

Family Dinner Night: Sunday Roast

The family table on a Sunday night is a sacred space. It marks the transition from the end of the weekend, when you hopefully got to soak up as much time together as possible, to turning your attention toward conquering the week ahead. It's almost like a team huddle—getting everyone pumped up for what's to come and offering your support to one another as you stare down the business ahead. Because we're about to launch headfirst into the hectic chaos of the week, I like to create a calm, relaxing environment to ease our way forward. I make sure that as a family we slow down, maybe shutting off our electronics a little earlier than usual, so we can really relish spending these last few peaceful moments together. Sunday nights are also special because you can take a bit more time and care with the meals you prepare: long-simmered stews or sauces, lazily braised veggies or meats, or, my favorite, Roasted Lamb with Mint Vinaigrette and Drippings-Roasted Sweet Potatoes (recipe follows). It's cozy enough for a laid-back Sunday afternoon in the kitchen but light enough for enjoying in spring. And I love how it calls to mind a traditional British Sunday roast—a ritual of gathering with friends and family (no matter how mixed and matched they've become) and celebrating the week.

roasted lamb with mint vinaigrette and drippings-roasted sweet potatoes

This is a seriously simple—but seriously impressive—dish that Bingham's dad, Matt, would often make for us. The potatoes have that soft-crispy thing going on and soak up all the lamb's juices as it roasts. The dish doesn't need much more in terms of flavor, but a bright mint vinaigrette ties everything together.

SERVES 8

For the roasted lamb and potatoes

One 4-pound leg of lamb

1 head garlic, cloves
    separated but not peeled

½ bunch fresh rosemary

½ bunch fresh sage

Zest of 1 lemon

Olive oil

Salt, to taste

Freshly ground black
    pepper, to taste

3 pounds sweet potatoes,
    cut into 1-inch pieces

For the mint vinaigrette

3 tablespoons chopped
    fresh mint

MAKE THE LAMB AND ROASTED POTATOES: Remove the lamb from the fridge 1 hour before you want to cook it and let it come to room temperature.

Preheat the oven to 400°F.

Peel 3 cloves of garlic and crush them with the side of your knife. Place them in a small bowl and set aside. Take half the rosemary sprigs, strip the needles, and combine them with half of the sage. Give the herbs a rough chop and add them to the bowl with the garlic. Add the lemon zest and a good lug of oil (as the British say), mix together, and set aside.

Season the lamb with salt and pepper, then drizzle with the marinade. Use your hands to slather it all over the meat. Place the lamb on the rack of a roasting pan and place in the oven. Cook for 1 hour 15 minutes, if you want it pink, or 1 hour 30 minutes, if you like it more well done.

Meanwhile, prep the potatoes, which will join the lamb for the final 30 minutes of cooking. Place the potatoes in a medium pot and add just enough cold water to cover. Add a generous pinch of salt and bring to a boil. Cook for 10 minutes and drain. Let them sit for a couple of minutes to cool slightly. Return the potatoes to the pot and toss in the remaining rosemary sprigs, sage, and whole garlic cloves. Season with salt and pepper and drizzle generously with oil. Toss just to coat, then carefully add the potatoes to the hot roasting pan beneath the lamb to catch the juices. Cook for 30 minutes, or until the potatoes are browned and crispy on the outside but tender and creamy in the middle. If they start looking a little too dark, carefully remove the potatoes using a slotted spoon and set aside while the lamb continues cooking. Remove the lamb from the oven and allow it to rest for 15 minutes before serving. If you haven't already done so, strain the potatoes from the drippings into a bowl and set aside.

MAKE THE MINT VINAIGRETTE: Whisk together the mint, vinegar, honey, shallot, Dijon, garlic, and salt. Continue whisking as you slowly stream in the olive oil. Adjust the seasoning with salt to taste.

Place the lamb on a platter surrounded by the potatoes and slice tableside, offering the mint vinaigrette on the side. Or slice the lamb in the kitchen and arrange the slices (about $1/2$ to 1 inch thick) on a platter before scattering the potatoes around the lamb. Serve drizzled with the mint vinaigrette.

1 tablespoon white wine vinegar

2 teaspoons honey

1 teaspoon minced shallot

1 teaspoon Dijon mustard

½ small garlic clove, minced

¼ teaspoon salt, plus more to taste

¼ cup extra-virgin olive oil

Give light
and people will
find the way.

—Ella Baker

TRANSFORMING
A SPACE

There's a reason people loved coming to our house when I was grow-ing up, and it's the same reason people love coming to my house now: it all has to do with *energy,* or how someone feels when they're there (i.e., welcome, comfortable, secure, taken care of). What contributes to that is: 1) your energy as a host—is it warm? Relaxed? Gracious? Is there inten-tion behind it? And 2) the energy you create in your home. It has nothing to do with how big your house is, how fancy your furniture, or how enormous your television. In fact, some of the most enjoyable gatherings I've been to were in teeny-tiny spaces that felt super lived in and *anything* but extravagant. I know it sounds all very California, but contrary to what most people think I've lived many places in the world, like New York and London, and I've found that no matter where you are that there are certain elements that take a space to a whole different level in terms of an inviting, cozy vibe—small touches that make guests feel like they're truly welcome to be there. No matter the scale or intention of a party—close-knit or straight-up crazy—these details go just as far in their effect.

✴ Lighting: Once when we were older teenagers, my brother and I had a party when we thought my parents were out of town for work. We had all of our friends at the house, and what was supposed to be ten or fifteen people turned into fifty kids packed into our living room. Well, as soon as things started getting going, the front door swung open, and in walked my mom. She didn't say a word, just looked at all of us and then up at the ceiling. She dimmed the lights and said, "Kids, if you're gonna have a party, lighting is *everything*." And she just walked away. Our friends were all shocked, thinking, *Your mom is the coolest!* My brothers and I knew she may not be so cool in the morning, but yeah, she had a point!

Especially for nighttime gatherings, a room that has bright, harsh lighting isn't cozy. Low lighting, on the other hand, helps people feel like they can let their hair down a little bit, like no one's watching. The best lighting is warm and soft and comes from different sources, especially lamps and candles (there should be at least one candle burning and one lamp lit in every room that you want guests to be in). You want the rooms to glow.

✴ Color and theme: A color scheme or themed favors are what tell your guests that they're in the right place. It can just be an arrangement of flowers, a candy-scape or color-coordinated treats, balloons, table décor, themed food or beverages, or a collection of party favors. These touches not only create ambience but also indicate that it's a place where people are meant to gather. A great trick for getting people to spread out in your home, or even sit in that fancy-looking chair that everyone's afraid to touch, is to use elements of the party to let them know they're welcome to stay: a dish of olives or nuts and a scattering of confetti on a table next to that intimidating chair, a banner and bundle of balloons in a corner that might not otherwise attract minglers, or setting up the food outside and the bar inside to encourage flow between the two spaces.

* **Something living**: A natural element, whether it's flowers, plants, feathers, eggs, or branches, adds a soft, comforting wavelength to a space. Being surrounded by plants—even tiny succulents or potted herbs—has a calming effect, and besides being an easy way to make a space look pretty and feel inviting, plants can actually make people *happier*. Researchers have found that living things in a space can also help people connect more deeply, feel a heightened sense of wellness and a reduced sense of stress, and have a generally sunnier outlook on life.[9] Not bad for a few little plants!

Especially when it comes to floral touches, there's no need to spend a ton. Put individual flowers in bud vases or fill a larger vase with just one flower you love. I also love using fresh herbs, either in arrangements or on top of each place setting. They're not only beautiful and natural looking, but they also lend a subtle earthy aroma (see also Scent below).

* **Something personal**: Artifacts from your life make a space feel lived in, like "life happens here," which in turn makes guests feel like they don't have to walk on eggshells. My favorite way to accomplish this is by having framed photographs scattered throughout my celebration space, in addition to trinkets and treasures I've collected in my travels.

* **Scent**: We experience a space with all our senses—including smell. I have at least one scented candle burning in my house at all times when I am awake, because I love how it instantly adds another layer of nuanced coziness, like a little subconscious welcome mat. I'll even cycle through a few different signature scents depending on the season, going with something light and bright in the warmer months and musky and deep in the colder ones. I'm not talking about an overpowering synthetic scent, though. Invest in high-quality 100 percent soy or beeswax candles, incense, or an essential oil diffuser that offers just a hint of smell—like a little background music. Here are some scents to consider, depending on the vibe you want:

  > CALMING: bergamont, chamomile, frankincense, lavender, lemon, myrrh, sweet melissa, vanilla, violet, ylang ylang, green tea

  > SEXY: jasmine, rose, cinnamon, neroli, patchouli, white ginger

  > UPLIFTING: cypress, rosemary, sage, grapefruit, mint, orange blossom, geranium, cucumber, fresh-cut grass, birch bark, vetiver

  > COZY: cloves, pine, cedar, eucalyptus, nutmeg, tobacco, sandalwood, fig, nag champa, wood fire, moss

* **Crystals**: I have crystals *everywhere*—large and small, as votives, as coasters, and as pieces of gorgeous earthy art. I believe that they hold energy and that certain ones are great for making spaces feel particularly inviting. Some of my favorites:

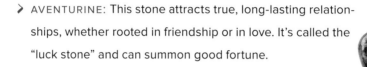

> AMETHYST: A soothing, calming stone that's rebalancing and restorative. People say it helps them feel watched over.

> AVENTURINE: This stone attracts true, long-lasting relationships, whether rooted in friendship or in love. It's called the "luck stone" and can summon good fortune.

> ROSE QUARTZ: Another comforting stone, but this one operates on the heart wavelength. Rose quartz symbolizes love and harmony and emits peaceful vibrations.

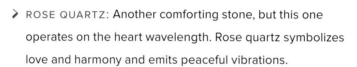

> TIGER'S-EYE: This "watchful" stone looks over your home as a guardian. It's also great for unblocking creative energy.

> ONYX: Black onyx is also known as a protection stone because it absorbs negative energy and transforms it into strength, vitality, and stamina. It's particularly valuable during times of stress or overwhelm.

> CLEAR QUARTZ: Considered the master of all healing crystals, quartz can magnify the vibrations of other stones. It can also help clear the mind of negativity, open the channels of communication, and deepen your connection with the natural world.

* **Cozy blankets**: There's nothing that says "nest here" more than a soft throw laid luxuriously across a chair or sofa. Nine times out of ten, if there's a blanket in the room during one of my parties, someone—if not multiple people—ends up under it.

* **Pillows, cushions and beanbags**: Fill your space with comfortable places for your guests to sit, lounge, rest, and gather. Make them feel like they can get cozy and tuck in for a long night of great company and conversation. Of course, if you are planning a dance party or a more formal affair you may want to rethink this, but be sure everyone has somewhere to perch.

* **Other inviting touches**: It might seem obvious, but just having entertaining-related items around makes people feel more welcome, whether or not you're actually having a party. It's a bar table with pretty glasses and coasters, lots of drink options in the fridge and snacks in the pantry, or rolled-up towels by the pool. If you are hosting a gathering, make things feel abundant. A table with a few dips and a bunch of veggie options looks more inviting than just hummus and carrots. A big tub spilling over with ice, beer, and sparkling waters looks great and makes people want to help themselves, rather than if the drinks were hidden in the fridge. These kinds of touches make people feel welcome, cared for, and happy to be celebrating with you.

SUMMER

Fourth of July
Lawn Chair Cookout

Oh man, Fourth of July. It just doesn't get much more fun. It's all about being outside: the kids running around like lunatics; the adults sipping on some tasty, refreshing cocktails; everyone loading up plates of food hot off the grill and just hanging out together. And yes, even amid all these quintessential party moments, there's a deeper reason to celebrate: we get to reflect on home and country, and how grateful we are for the freedoms that we have. It's also a moment to pause and give a little thought to how our year is going—and where it's going next. So often these things get lost in the shuffle between planning what's on the menu and decking out the kids' bikes for the parade. Before planning your Fourth, revisit your Drawing Board and think about what this holiday means to you. Is it a valuable opportunity for you to spend time with your friends or extended family, since you normally don't get to during the busy summer? Are you celebrating that you finally get to play, thanks to a much-needed long weekend? Is it officially saying happy birthday to our country? Let the true meaning of the holiday for you shine through in your plans.

I like taking the traditional patriotic vibe to a whole new place. I go all out with decorations in the essential red, white, and blue—balloons, bunting, flags of all sizes—and then tie in tons of other bright colors so that everyone's feeling festive. I also like changing things up with an unexpected theme, like having everyone bring their lawn chairs for a quirky backyard bash that lets everyone get a little creative.

For me, Fourth of July embraces easy fun. Since it falls mid-summer, we often find ourselves celebrating this holiday on vacation, or going on vacation to celebrate. On the East Coast, the Fourth is when the ocean finally feels warm enough to swim in. The days are long and hot, and we just need a reason to have a party. I love it. This one is all low-stress, kid-focused fun.

Do It Right

BYO LAWN CHAIRS

Get your guests into the spirit of all things America by having them bring their own lawn chairs—the more obnoxiously decked out with streamers, balloons, glitter, and posters, the better. Set up picnic blankets on the lawn for people to group their chairs around and for anyone who needs an extra spot to lounge, then put out lots of buckets of ice for beer and sodas and baskets of chips and other munchies, so everyone can just sprawl out and hunker down. And definitely don't forget a playlist packed with songs about the good ol' U.S. of A.: Tom Petty's "American Girl," Bruce Springsteen's "Born in the U.S.A.," Simon and Garfunkel's "America," Don McLean's "American Pie"—you get the idea!

Other things to bundle up in baskets:

* Baseballs, footballs, and whiffle balls
* Sunscreen and parasols (especially if they clip onto the lawn chairs!)
* Flip-flops and towels, for the pool, sprinklers, or hose
* Personalized beer koozies and sun visors or baseball caps
* American flags

Do It Light

Because balance is key, especially after a big, juicy burger!

the hudson pucker

I came up with this version of a margarita-lemonade mash-up because I wanted the refreshing flavor of lemonade without all the sugar, and a festive cocktail option that didn't involve a lot of ingredients. All this drink calls for is lemon, honey, and añejo or aged tequila, which has the same clean-buzz benefits of pure-agave tequila, plus a little more body and smokiness to it.

It's so simple that it doesn't even require a proper recipe, just a quick how-to:

Fill a tumbler about a quarter of the way full with fresh-squeezed lemon juice. Stir in a teaspoon of honey and a shot of tequila (I get pretty generous here), and then add a good handful of ice. If you want to get all fancy with it, add the lemon juice and honey to a shaker and shake until the honey is dissolved. Don't forget to add the honey to the lemon before you add the ice or the honey won't dissolve. Also, I like to make a big batch of the honey and lemon mix ahead of time so you can keep the puckers flowing! Then add the ice and tequila and shake until chilled. Garnish it up with strawberries and blueberries to give it a patriotic touch.

pretty damn good burger

Is there anything else you'd serve at a Fourth of July party?! This is my signature version that includes a secret ingredient: onion soup mix. My grandma would add the store-bought kind to her famous brisket because it adds all kinds of rich, savory, spiced-up yumminess. In order to not totally wreck your sodium count and avoid mystery ingredients, this recipe calls for making your own homemade mix. I've also added my own twist with a Worcestershire and Bragg Liquid Aminos combo, which adds even more savory depth of flavor; plus a heaping handful of chopped greens. I assure you, no one will be able to taste the difference—especially the kids—but they'll reap all its vitamin-packed goodness. I've also included instructions for how to turn this mega burger into smaller sliders, which is great for little ones or if you want to put these out as part of a spread for game night, Football Sunday, or any other nibble-worthy occasion.

Serve these with plenty of veggie topping options like shredded lettuce or cabbage, sliced tomatoes and onions, pickles—both classic dill and other varities like carrots, hot peppers, and onions—roasted red peppers, or even kimchi. And definitely don't forget the staples: ketchup, mustard (yellow and stone-ground), and mayo.

**MAKES 8 LARGE BURGERS
OR 12 SLIDERS**

¼ cup dried onion flakes

1 teaspoon salt

1 teaspoon pepper

¼ teaspoon onion powder

¼ teaspoon parsley flakes

¼ teaspoon paprika

⅛ teaspoon celery seed

2 pounds ground beef
(80 percent lean and
20 percent fat)

1 packed cup kale or
spinach leaves, finely
chopped

½ cup breadcrumbs

1 egg

1 tablespoon
Worcestershire sauce

1 tablespoons Bragg's
Liquid Aminos

Canola or vegetable oil

8 brioche hamburger buns
or 12 slider buns, sliced
in half

Veggies and condiments for
serving

pretty damn good burger (continued)

Preheat your grill to high heat. Brush the grates with oil to keep the burgers from sticking.

In a small bowl, combine the onion flakes, salt, pepper, onion powder, parlsey flakes, celery seed, and paprika. Set aside.

In a large bowl, combine the beef, kale or spinach, bread-crumbs, egg, Worcestershire sauce, and Liquid Aminos. Use your hands to mix until just combined—don't overmix or you'll end up with tough burgers. If making large burg-ers, shape the meat into 8 patties, about ¾-inch thick. If making sliders, form the meat into 12 patties, about 2 inches wide and ¾ inches thick. Grill the large patties for about 5 minutes, flip, then another 3 minutes for me-dium. For sliders, cook for 4 minutes, flip, and cook for another 4 to 6 minutes for medium. Cook longer if you prefer them more well done. Transfer the burgers to a platter and cover with foil.

Lay the buns cut-side down on the grill and toast until grill marks have just formed, about 1 minute.

Layer up the buns with a patty and your toppings of choice; serve 'em while they're hot!

boozy berries

One of the best things about summer is the amazing fruit that's in season. Even though we Californians get pretty spoiled with our year-round bounty, there's nothing like the berries at the market this time of year. They're so deliciously syrupy and sweet on their own that they don't need a lot of fuss to make them the perfect light dessert. All you need to do is mound the berries in a bowl and sprinkle them with the tiniest bit of sugar and lemon juice, which will draw out their juices and soften up the fruit, almost as though they've been baked. If you want, you could also add a drizzle of Grand Marnier, an orange-flavored liqueur, for a sophisticated finish, or you could leave it out altogether. This dish is pretty enough to put out as is, or you can layer up the berries parfait-style with whipped cream (as a yummy dairy-free alternative, try coconut milk whipped cream) in mason jars or glasses.

Put the berries in a large bowl and sprinkle with the sugar, lemon juice and zest, and Grand Marnier, if using. Toss gently to combine. Let the berries sit at room temperature for at least 1 hour or refrigerate in a covered container for up to 3 days. Serve topped with freshly whipped cream, or alternately layer the fruit and whipped cream for a parfait.

If you don't want your berries boozy, use coconut sugar instead of grand marnier. Just as delish and good for everyone.

SERVES 10

5 cups assorted berries
   (blueberries, strawberries,
   raspberries, blackberries),
   washed
1 to 2 tablespoons sugar
Juice and zest of 1 lemon
1/4 cup Grand Marnier
   (optional)
Whipped coconut milk
   cream, for serving

Do It Easy

READY-IN-A-MINUTE SIDES

Summertime sides are some of the quickest and easiest to pull together, especially if you're showcasing barely-mussed-with, fresh-from-the-market produce. Here's a few beyond simple crowd-pleasers:

Cubed Cantaloupe and Honeydew + Feta + Basil or Mint + Olive Oil

Charred Corn Kernels + Mayo + Cotija Cheese + Lime Juice + Cilantro

Heirloom Tomatoes + Burrata or Mozzarella + Olive Oil and Balsamic Vinegar

Cooked Baby Potatoes + Bacon + Dill + Mustard Vinaigrette

Shaved Summer Squash + Arugula + Ricotta + Toasted Nuts + Olive Oil and Champagne Vinegar

OR, go BYO! Ask guests to bring their favorite side or dessert, along with their lawn chair. Have a friend whose deviled eggs are killer? Or who nails the cobbler every time? Don't be shy about making requests! You could also make it a continuation of your theme—ask people to bring their favorite hometown cookout dish or their favorite road trip eats.

DON'T FORGET THE FIREWORKS

Whether you are at the beach, in a local park, or in your own backyard, a Fourth of July party should be a let-your-hair-down, no-fuss, all-fun, flip-flops-and-floppy-hats kind of day. Get outside, enjoy the sun (but don't forget the sunscreen!), light up the grill, and grab your favorite grown-up beverage. As I said, this holiday comes just when we need a celebration, complete with fireworks! Even when you're having this much fun, don't forget to appreciate everything that freedom means to you.

All-the-Kids Birthday Party

There is nothing more special than a child's birthday. Aside from it being a time when we as parents need to confront the fact that our babies are growing up *way* too fast, it's when we get to put the birthday boy or girl up on a pedestal, shower them with every drop of love we have to give, and let them soak up all that happiness and joy while we celebrate the things that make him or her unique. That's why in our house birthdays are a whole-family affair, even if that means younger bro and his friends get to crash older bro's party. It used to be one thing to plan a party for the kids when they were little, when all I had to do to blow their minds was to invite their buddies, order a cute cake, put up a bunch of balloons, and maybe arrange for an appearance from their favorite superhero. It didn't take much to win Mom of the Year back then! But when my oldest son turned thirteen, I knew it was going to be a very different story—no more silly games and cutesy themes for this guy. And yet, I still wanted to make the party fun for the six-year-olds who would be in attendance. I decided that I needed to give each kid—and the adults—space to do something that felt inclusive and festive. It was a challenge, but I realized that planning Ryder's birthday now is even more special, because it gives us the perfect opportunity to connect with each other and talk about what he likes, what his interests are, and what he'd like to do with

his friends. I get to learn even more about the people in his life he cares about and, ultimately, what makes him happy. Then I layer in activities and treats for the younger set to enjoy—and completely destroy.

FOR THE TOO-COOL-FOR-SCHOOL TWEEN OR TEEN

When it comes to planning a party for an older kid, make sure you're involving them in the process, from the theme to the food to the entertainment—and don't forget what it was like to be their age. You'll be surprised how even the most standoffish tween or teen warms up to the idea of a party tailor-made for them.

How to win cool-mom points:

* **Designate separate areas of the house for the kids and the adults.** It will give the kids the feeling that they're still being chaperoned—but aren't being watched. Ask what part of the house your kid wants to take over: Should you clear out the furniture in the living room to make a dance floor? Create a hangout around a backyard bonfire? The pool? Or make the basement the chill spot? Then pick another area for parents to hang in the meantime, with some drinks and light snacks on offer.

* **Music, music, music.** Make it your kid's homework to put together a playlist. I guarantee you'll end up hearing at least three new bands you'll want to start listening to.

* **Find out the cool eats.** There's something about kids this age and their oddly trendy food, what everyone's going off campus to get. For me it was Chin Chin potstickers and BBQ chicken pizza from California Pizza Kitchen. For Ryder, it's energy drinks and Takis, these neon-orange flavored tortilla chips. Ask your kid; stock up. Even if it's total junk, it's just one day. Put out trays and bowls of things to eat on every table and surface; it'll help the kids feel like the party space is their place to be.

* **Consider bringing in some entertainment.** Rent a karaoke machine or hire a badass PG-13 magician.

* **Set up a bar—a soda bar.** Just like you'd display booze for adults, arrange a bar cart or table with retro glass bottles of soda or different types of canned drinks.

* **Decorate with string lights and lanterns instead of balloons for a more grown-up, festive vibe.**

FOR THE TAGALONG
YOUNGER BROTHER OR SISTER

It's no secret that if you throw a bunch of kids in a room with balloons, streamers, and sugary treats they're going to have a blast. It doesn't take a whole lot for the ten-and-under crowd to let the birthday spirit move them! But you also want to make sure that they're in a space that's suited for them (read: can be totally and utterly torn apart) and is engaging enough to keep them busy when the time comes to give the older kids some space. Here's how to make sure no one feels like they're missing out on the fun:

* **Make it a conversation:** Ask your little one where he or she wants to be during the festivities and make sure their choice is heard by the birthday boy or girl. Of course, the guest of honor gets first dibs, but try not to let little bro or sis feel like they're being pushed out of the way. If negotiations break down, offering to turn the little one's bedroom into a super-secret birthday party hideout, complete with wall-to-wall decorations, is usually hard to pass up.

* **Make it perfectly imperfect:** Any decorations that go into this room are liable to be pulled on, swung from, and otherwise manhandled. An easy and inexpensive way to deck out the mini-party is by floating balloons on the ceiling and tying them to just about anything—Chairs! Tables! Lamps! Toys! Hang streamers from every surface possible (channel your high school toilet-papering days) to complete the vibe.

* **Add activities:** Instead of shelling out for extra entertainment, stock the room with fun things for the kids to do: instruments for them to play (Bing loves to show off his drum skills!), a pinata (with adult supervision, please!), pin the tail on the Darth Vader, or a special arts

and crafts project, like having everyone chip in to make a Happy Birthday banner to hang on the wall.

* **Keep bellies full:** Make sure there's plenty of snacks to both fuel the fun and to get something into the kids besides sugar. Stick with easy-to-make options that are kid-friendly classics like turkey tortilla rollups, chips and pretzels, carrots and hummus, fruit kebabs, mini grilled cheese sandwiches, or sunflower butter and jellies. While I don't usually let my boys get too sugared up, birthdays are an exception. Fill the room with jars of colorful candy like lollipops, Pixy Sticks, jellybeans, licorice, and M&M's.

BRING EVERYONE TOGETHER

For the big finish to the party, invite everyone to come from their respective celebration corners and enjoy an ice cream feast. There's no better way to bring people together than overheaping DIY sundaes. Set up a table with two to three different ice cream flavors (basic is best here—vanilla, chocolate, strawberry) and *tons* of topping options: candy bars; giant cookies; chocolate-covered fruit and nuts; sprinkles; pretzels; sliced bananas, cherries, and strawberries; hot fudge; caramel sauce; marshmallow fluff; whipped cream. The presentation should be just as impressive as the spread—you want it to feel like a confectionary dreamscape! Break out all your cake stands to create dramatic tiers, plus platters, bowls, and jars to showcase the topping options. Serve with oversized spoons and embrace all the inevitable drips and dribbles.

Do It Right

MEANINGFUL TOUCHES

* Analog Photo Booth: For a fun activity that doubles as decoration (and a gift for your child), buy an inexpensive Polaroid camera with lots of film, along with colorful paper and pens. Hang a big board on the wall where all the kids can tack up their snaps, plus any messages they want to write to the birthday boy or girl, or any words they'd use to describe him or her. Throw in some crazy glasses, hats, tiaras, beads, and other accessories that they can wear for the photo session.

* A Greater-Good-y Bag: Consider actually doing a favor instead of sending one home with your guests. Sit down with your child and help him choose three charities that he'd like to donate to as part of his celebration. Create posters with a description of each one and hang them on the wall. Place a jar below each poster. Then give the party guests envelopes containing a small amount of cash (the same amount you'd otherwise spend on junky trinkets for a goody bag) and ask them to put their money in the jar or jars of their choice. You could also include a note on the invitation that says, "Yes, we love presents, but in addition [or instead], kindly bring $5/$10 to donate to my son's/ daughter's favorite charities." It's such a great way to teach your kids how important it is to give back.

Backyard Tournament Pop-Up Party

Growing up, my brothers and I spent our summers on a lake in Northern Ontario. During the long afternoons when we were there, it was often pretty quiet. We had to work to keep ourselves entertained. So we invented the Muskoka Olympics, a tournament that consisted of games like a beanbag toss, Ping-Pong (and, eventually, beer pong). When you share a house with three brothers, these kinds of games become a regular part of your life and the competition can get intense, but these tournaments created some of my favorite memories. Now they're one of the first things I think about when the weather starts to heat up, when you can't imagine spending time anywhere but outside. That's when I call for a Backyard Tournament Pop-Up Party.

This is definitely a don't-lift-a-finger kind of gathering. No decorations, no themes, no big deal. Just fun! Arrange a potluck for food, or if even that feels like too much work, order in. Think foods that you can eat with your hands (no need for silverware or plates—done!): ribs, wings, dumplings, sliders, subs.

If you have the space in your backyard, set up camp there, and if you don't, consider packing it up for a park, the beach, or even your stoop if you live in the city—a beanbag toss will definitely fit on the sidewalk! Then take stock of what kind of game gear you have on hand, organize teams—the more evenly split, the better the competition—and play! If there are enough kids participating, you can divide them into their own teams and have the adults play a separate game, or have everyone play together—it's a win-win.

What I love most about this pop-up party, aside from the fact that you can't get caught up in your head about whether there's enough to eat or drink or if anyone will come, is that it's major spirit food. What I mean by that is that play is a very powerful force when it comes to our overall wellness. Exercise is, of course, good for our bodies and minds (it reduces stress; improves attention and memory; boosts energy and stamina; increases longevity; strengthens our bones, heart, and skin; and makes us feel more alive), but *play* takes it to a whole new level. When we let down our walls and quiet the voice inside that tells us things like "You'll look stupid" or "Act your age," we can reconnect with our inner child, that same spontaneous little girl or boy who ran free, dove head-first down the slip 'n' slide, or hung upside down for what felt like hours from the monkey bars. Play feeds the body *and* the soul; it opens the mind *and* the heart. When we can let go of control and stop judging ourselves, we open ourselves up to more pleasure in all its many forms. And that, my friends, is a really good thing.

It is no bad thing to celebrate a simple life.

—J.R.R. Tolkien

Father's Day Picnic

Just like Mother's Day, Father's Day is one of the most significant holidays, to my mind. It's of course for celebrating all things Dad—what he likes to eat, how he likes to relax, his favorite socks/underwear/ties—but it's also a time to honor the man who helped put down roots for your family. It doesn't matter if he's not your biological father or the one who married your mother first; if there's a man in your life whose guidance and strength have held you up, then he's the man of the hour. While I think every day is a great time to give thanks to your parents, this is one day when you can go all out and let Dad know that you've been thinking about him.

Since Father's Day falls right at the beginning of summer when the weather isn't overbearingly hot, try getting the family outside for some active together time. As I mentioned in the previous section, the benefits of being out in the fresh air and moving your body are vast. There's really no better gift that we can give ourselves or our families. I say pack up a picnic basket full of Dad's favorite munchies and take it to a spot that's meaningful to him: a clearing by his favorite hiking path that you can enjoy after a walk, a park that you all can ride bikes to, a beach where you can all brush up on your surfing or paddleboarding skills, or the backyard (hey, some guys just love their yard!) to throw around a football or baseball.

I also like the idea of taking an otherwise casual summer picnic and turning it up a couple of notches. Think coordinating picnic blankets (sheets and tablecloths work well here), cloth napkins, enamelware plates and serving platters (the *best* investment if you like packing up a meal to go, and also so handsome on a buffet table), and (plastic) wine or cocktail glasses. Pack a couple of large mason jars or carafes with drinks—maybe one with pre-mixed warm-weather cocktails, like gin and tonics, Pimm's Cups, or Dark 'n' Stormies, and another with citrus- or cucumber-infused water. Also consider bringing along a few platters or wood boards to display the food and to balance drinks on.

Make sure you involve other family members in the planning so they can put together their own special baskets—and also share the load. You're not exactly packing light for this picnic!

Do It Right

CARD IN A JAR

Instead of going the usual route of buying your dad some sappy, impersonal card from the store, invite everyone to write down their favorite thing about him on a piece of card stock, whether it's "You're dependable" or "I love knowing I can always beat you at golf." Put the sentiments in a simple glass jar and let Dad go through them at your picnic.

Do It Easy

The best food for a picnic is anything that can be made ahead of time, parceled up, and kept at room temperature. And to me, nothing says picnic like family-sized sandwiches. All you need to do is layer up a few fresh baguettes with different ingredient combinations—sweet and savory—then wrap them with parchment and twine. Here are a few of my favorite combos:

Ham + Gruyère + Butter

Turkey + Avocado + Pickled Onions

Pesto + Tomatoes + Mozzarella

Roast Beef + Cheddar + Caramelized Onions

Grilled Broccoli Rabe + Sausage

Roasted Veggies + Tapenade + Hummus

Italian Salami + Provolone + Oil and Vinegar

Nutella + Bananas

Almond Butter + Jam + Granola

As for sides, consider a selection of grain or pasta salads, like farro, quinoa, or penne tossed with chopped raw or roasted veggies, olives or marinated artichokes, feta or goat cheese, and a vinaigrette or pesto. Other good options include grilled vegetables dressed with sea salt, olive oil, and a little citrus zest; simple skewers like melon and prosciutto or watermelon, feta, and mint; and a bundle of whatever seasonal fruit looks good at the market. Either pack up these items in larger cardboard boxes so everyone can enjoy family-style, or give each person his or her individually portioned box.

Back-to-School Taco Night

If there's one dinner that's constantly requested in my house, it's taco night. My kids—and any friends who have experienced this evening—cannot get enough of the chewy-crispy corn tortillas stuffed with spiced beef (or refried beans) and basically any topping known to mankind. The thing about taco night is that if you're going to do tacos, you gotta *do* tacos, which means a full-time job working the stove, frying up tortillas so they're hot and fresh— nothing like the soggy, grease-soaked ones you get from takeout. While that may not sound like fun, that's where you are wrong! Taco night means you just have to bring the fun to you! Which is usually no problem—I've found that the party usually ends up in the kitchen whenever there's something delicious smelling on the stove. It ends up being a super-casual setting where everyone's just hanging out, enjoying one another's company.

I especially love hosting a taco night at the end of the summer, a couple of days before the boys go back to school. We invite over all the kids' friends and their parents, plus the cousins, aunts, uncles, and grandparents, so we can all reconnect after a long summer of constantly being on the go. It's a time when everyone can come back together, share what they've been up to that summer, and get back into the swing of regular routines. This feels particularly important for all the kids, because they're just starting to understand what it means for them to have their own tribe. Right now that might be only a group of people their age who like the same things they do, but over time, that will evolve into deeper relationships. And when they look back at who has been in their lives to share in all the special moments—not just birthdays and holidays—I hope they'll be able to picture the table that we were all sitting around and realize that's what we were doing there. That and, of course, eating as many tacos as humanly possible.

Do It Right

SUMMER APPRECIATION CIRCLE

Going back to school at the end of summer is when kids reconnect with one another after a long, busy vacation. It's also typically the first time in a while that we've seen our friends and family, since everyone usually scatters, especially in August. Reflecting on the summer and sharing something you appreciated the most is not only a great conversation starter and a fun way to catch everyone up on what you've been doing the past few months, but it's also a nice way to mark the end of the season and get ready for the next chapter. Go around the room or table and have everyone contribute one thing: A great surfing trip? Winning the baseball championship? Finally mastering an ollie at the skate park? It doesn't need to be deep and philosophical, just sincere. Your kids might not be waxing poetic about summer coming to a close and what that means for the rhythm of their lives, but by creating this moment, you're helping to put them in touch with the part of them that recognizes the importance of taking a beat, tuning in, and connecting.

Do It Easy

tacos with all the good stuff

My first taco night secret is the tortillas—they've *gotta* be corn and they've *gotta* be good. Flour tortillas are just not what we're talking about here, nor are we talking about any kind of healthy-ish alternative. Do yourself a favor and just go with the best-quality corn tortillas you can find.

The second secret is balancing the homemade with the store-bought. I always make a souped-up spiced ground meat filling that's next-level delicious. But the toppings, those I leave to the store: refried beans, lettuce, chopped tomatoes and onions, cabbage slaw, a variety of salsas, Mexican-style cheeses, guacamole and sliced avocado, pickled onions and jalapeños—anything that anybody would want on a taco. Get the kids involved by having them help put everything in cute little bowls and arranging them on the table.

The third secret? Embrace the kitchen hangout. Making tacos means babysitting the stove. By the time you've fried up one big batch of crispy, chewy tortillas and put them out for everyone, it's usually time to head back and start round two—because no one eats just one. It's not hard work by any stretch; it just means this isn't the party where you're hanging on the couch with your friends. So bring the party to you in the kitchen: Set out a bunch of snacks, give everyone a job to do, put together a little bar station, and definitely make sure there's music.

In a small bowl, combine the chili powder, cumin, paprika, onion powder, salt, and pepper.

Heat the oil in a large skillet over medium-high heat. Add the onion and cook until soft and lightly brown around the edges, 5 to 6 minutes.

Add the beef and cook, breaking up the meat with your spoon so it's finely crumbled, until browned, 4 to 6 minutes. Stir in the spice mixture and cook for 1 minute. Pour

SERVES 8 TO 12

2 tablespoons chili powder

1 tablespoon ground cumin

2 teaspoons cornstarch

2 teaspoons salt, plus more
   to taste

1 teaspoon oregano, dried
   or fresh

1 teaspoon paprika

tacos with all the good stuff (continued)

1 teaspoon onion powder

1 teaspoon celery salt

½ teaspoon cayenne pepper
(omit if you're not going
for spicy)

½ teaspoon red pepper
flakes (omit if you're not
going for spicy)

¼ teaspoon freshly ground
black pepper, plus more
to taste

2 tablespoons olive oil

1 medium yellow onion,
finely chopped

2 pounds ground beef chuck

¼ cup beef broth

Canola oil, for frying

20 (6-inch) corn tortillas

Plenty of paper towels!

in the broth and continue cooking for another 3 minutes. Turn off the heat and set aside.

In a small clean skillet, add enough canola oil to come about ½ inch up the side of the pan. Heat the oil over medium heat until it looks like it's shimmering, but not smoking. (If it's smoking, it's too hot.) For the easiest method: Lay a tortilla in the oil and fry for 10 seconds, flip, and fry for another 10. It should be chewy, not crispy. Transfer the tortilla to a paper towel-lined plate and sprinkle with salt. Continue with the remaining tortillas OR go for a more advanced taco shell technique: Using tongs, lay half of the tortilla flat in the oil, continuing to hold the other half with the tongs so you create a taco shell shape. Fry for 10 seconds, then lay the other half into the oil, holding the fried half with the tongs. Fry for 10 more seconds and transfer to a paper towel-lined plate. Don't worry if they're not perfect! They'll still be delicious. Sprinkle with salt and repeat with the remaining tortillas.

cinnamon-sugar tacos

Since you're already in the kitchen and you are already a tortilla-warming pro, you should definitely make this super-easy, super-fast dessert that my kids go nuts for.

Using tongs, heat a flour tortilla (tastier for sweet uses) directly over the flame of your stove—don't even bother with a pan—so the tortilla just begins to char at the edges for a tiny bit of burnt flavor. While the tortilla is warm, spread it with butter, sprinkle it with cinnamon and raw sugar, and roll it up like a cigar.

Family Dinner Night: Saturday Night In

Summer evenings are for grilling, full stop. So this is a family dinner idea that's great for staying in, but not cooped up inside. I love setting up DIY kebabs where everyone can make their own combos and have fun threading things on the skewers (maybe skip the handling of raw meat step for the little ones, but they can at least let you know what they want to eat). Then I marinate everything in a flavorful oil, throw it on the grill, and serve with a dipping sauce like a pesto, garlic-spiked yogurt, or muhammara, a spicy red pepper spread. It seriously takes no time at all. Go full-on Mediterranean mezze by putting out store-bought salads and spreads, like tabbouleh, baba ghanoush, and hummus, and lots of herb-and-oil-marinated goodies, like grilled peppers and eggplants, artichoke hearts, olives, and cubes of feta. Pita is definitely a must—especially brushed with olive oil and warmed over the fire. And if the grill is going, you might as well also throw on some halved stone fruit, like peaches and nectarines, for a smoky after-dinner treat. Silverware optional!

mix-and-match kebab 101

THE BASICS

* **Stick with proteins that are quick-cooking, tender, and won't dry out.** My favorites are sirloin tip, pork chops, chicken thighs, lamb, shrimp, and salmon.

* **Load up on veggies! Go with classics like bell peppers, onions (especially red onion, which gets caramelized and sweet), mushrooms, zucchini, and summer squash.** Then add fun, more unusual kebab options like cherry or grape tomatoes (so pretty), artichoke hearts, fennel, extra-firm tofu, and cubes of halloumi cheese and day-old bread.

* **If you're using wood skewers, make sure you soak them in water for 30 minutes before grilling—otherwise they'll burn!**

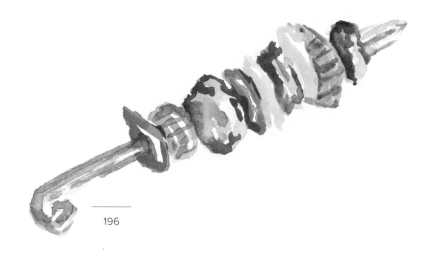

THE PREP

Slice all your ingredients into similar-sized pieces, about 1 to 1½ inches. Arrange all your ingredients in dishes or bowls for people to assemble their own variations. A pro tip I once got was to use two skewers for each kebab so that the food lies flat on the grill and cooks more evenly. Also suggest that people not tightly pack their skewers, since that can make the kebabs take a lot longer to cook. When everyone is done making their kebabs, give the skewers a soak in the All-the-Herbs Marinade (recipe on next page) for at least 1 hour.

THE GRILL

Arrange the kebabs on the grill over medium to high heat and cook for 10 to 15 minutes, rotating them every 2 or 3 minutes, until they're looking nice and charred and cooked through. Serve with pesto, tzatziki, or a simple Greek yogurt sauce (just combine yogurt, olive oil, lemon juice, and salt and pepper to taste; fresh herbs optional). Done!

all-the-herbs marinade

This super-simple marinade has a fresh-from-the-garden vibe, even if not a single sprig is from your backyard. A good rule of thumb is that you'll need about ½ cup of marinade per pound of meat.

Strip the herbs from their stems and place them in a blender. Add the garlic and olive oil, and pulse until the herbs and garlic are chopped. Add the lemon and orange juice and season with salt, pepper, and chili flakes to taste. Transfer the marinade to a large plastic zip-top baggie and add the kebabs. If you're using different kinds of meat, make a bag for each type, dividing the marinade among them. Make sure the kebabs are well coated and let them marinate in the fridge for 30 minutes to 1 hour, giving the bag(s) a shake or a turn every so often. If you're not using the marinade immediately, store it in the fridge for up to 2 days. When you're ready to grill, remove the kebabs from the marinade; discard the marinade.

MAKES ABOUT ¾ CUPS

4 sprigs rosemary
1 small bundle thyme
1 small bundle oregano
1 small bundle sage
4 cloves garlic, smashed
2 cups olive oil
2 tablespoons lemon juice
2 tablespoons orange juice
Kosher salt, to taste
Freshly ground black
    pepper, to taste
Red chili flakes, to taste

A PRETTY
STOCKED PANTRY

How to Be Ready for When Parties Just Happen

Some of the most memorable parties are the ones that come out of nowhere: when a warm afternoon turns into ten people hanging around in your backyard listening to music by the pool until dinner, or your date with the sofa turns into a crowd busting in to have an impromptu dance party. When this happens, you want to keep the mood feeling easy and free. But you can't keep the mood that way if you don't *feel* that way—remember Party Rule #7? The host should be having the most fun! If you are too stressed to relax, then your guests will certainly pick up on that. So how can you be party ready? How can you keep yourself open to a spur-of-the-moment gathering? One of the practical ways to be ready for a party on the fly is to keep your pantry stocked with versatile basics, whether it's to whip up a meal or put out a spread of things to snack on.

DINNER IN A MINUTE

I'm half Italian, so maybe that's why I feel so close to that culture's knack for turning a few humble ingredients into so many amazing meal options—namely onion, garlic, tomatoes, and olive oil. These are some of my go-to staples that, either on their own or with fresh veggies and proteins, will do the trick for a simple lunch or dinner.

* **Good-quality balsamic or red wine vinegar**: Shake this with a good-quality extra virgin olive oil, salt, and pepper for a quick dressing.

* **Canned cannellini beans**: Drain and puree the beans with olive oil, lemon juice, and salt for a quick spread, or toss with greens for a hearty salad.

* **Canned tomatoes**: Crushed up and cooked down with onion, garlic, olive oil, and salt—and even a handful of chopped veggies like eggplant or kale—and you've got a yummy sauce for pasta or grilled meat, veggies, fish, or even tofu. Add a glug of olive oil and a pinch of salt and puree, and you have pizza sauce.

* **Dried pasta and grains**: Quinoa, farro, wheatberries, rice, and any shape of dried pasta can easily be cooked and served as is or heaped with toppings and a

dressing: serve with roasted or raw veggies plus a sauce or a drizzle of olive oil, or toss with greens.

* **Fresh veg of choice**: I always have a head of broccoli in my crisper because my kids love it. Go with whatever option that your kids are into or you happen to have on hand. Serve it bite-sized and raw with dips, toss with olive oil and salt and either roast in the oven or toss on the grill, or cook and then puree it with olive oil and garlic for a quick dip or spread that's really yummy on pasta, grain salads, or pizza.

* **Frozen veggies**: Such a great alternative to fresh in a pinch. Most are frozen at peak freshness, so you're getting almost as much flavor as you would if you'd bought in season. Some of my favorites are corn (for tossing with jalapeño, cilantro, lime juice, olive oil, salt, and pepper for a quick salsa), cauliflower (for roasting until crisp and golden; just add olive oil, salt, and pepper), and sweet potatoes (bake until crispy on the outside and tender on the inside, serve as fries, done).

* **Garlic**: Everyone's favorite flavor booster! Use it raw and minced in dressings and sauces or toss it with cooked veggies. Or roast a whole head by wrapping it in foil and baking until the cloves are tender and golden. Spread the results on anything your heart desires with a pinch of sea salt!

* **Good-quality extra virgin olive oil**: Drizzle this over *everything*. Also use it as a base for a marinade with a squeeze of lemon or lime, a couple of cloves of garlic, and any fresh herbs you have on hand. Or for a quick fish preparation, season the fillet with salt and pepper, submerge it in oil, toss in whatever fresh herbs you have handy, and bake until the fish is flaky and cooked through.

* **Bacon or Pancetta**: Even though I don't regularly cook with red meat because I don't love the way it makes my body feel due to the inflammation it can cause, there's no denying that adding a bit of bacon or pancetta (bacon's Italian, unsmoked counterpart) to a dish every once in a while brings a whole new level of rich, satisfying flavor. Render out its lovely, smoky fat in a pan over very low heat and use the drippings as the base for a stew or to cook beans or sauté vegetables. Then sprinkle the crisped-up pieces over salads, soups, and pastas. Or add bread, lettuce, and tomato for a B(or P)LT. Just make sure you're buying a product that doesn't contain added sugars or preservatives like nitrates/nitrites, and comes from an animal that's been raised responsibly; it will say "pasture-raised" or "organic" on the label.

* **Lemons and limes:** A squeeze on sautéed veggies, a bed of greens, or just about anything else gives dishes more nuanced flavor without adding extra salt.

* **Loaf of good bread:** Slather with olive oil and toast it or give it a quick char on the grill. You can then slice and serve it alongside your main dish (with a schmear of dip for crostini) or top it with cheese, roasted vegetables, thinly sliced meats, and a drizzle of dressing for sandwiches. Or tear the loaf into bite-sized pieces; toss with oil, salt, and pepper; and brown in a pan for quick croutons. Give old bread new life by repurposing it as French toast or bread crumbs.

* **Olives, pickles, and other brined or cured things:** Olives (green, black, or kalamata), capers, cornichons, pickles, sauerkraut, oil-cured artichokes, and sun-dried tomatoes all add a nice salty zip to anything you add them to, whether chopped and tossed into salads, sprinkled on crostini or pizzas, or stirred into soups and stews. And they last pretty much forever in your fridge.

* **Onion**: Everyone's other favorite flavor booster. Chopped and raw, they add bite to salads, soups, and stews; slowly sautéed over low heat until thick and jammy, and they're decadent and sweet—perfect for topping pizzas, pastas, salads, sandwiches, soups, or proteins. Or slice them, brush them with olive oil, and lay them on the grill: smoky, caramelized perfection for layering with other grilled veggies or on sandwiches or burgers.

* **Parmesan cheese**: Get the good stuff, *not* the Frankenstein version you buy in the unrefrigerated section of the grocery store. It should come sliced, attached to a rind, and it will last pretty much forever in the fridge and adds a complex, salty finish to just about anything. Sprinkle it over salads, soups, or cooked veggies; add a grated handful to salad dressings; and definitely save the rinds to simmer in soups and sauces.

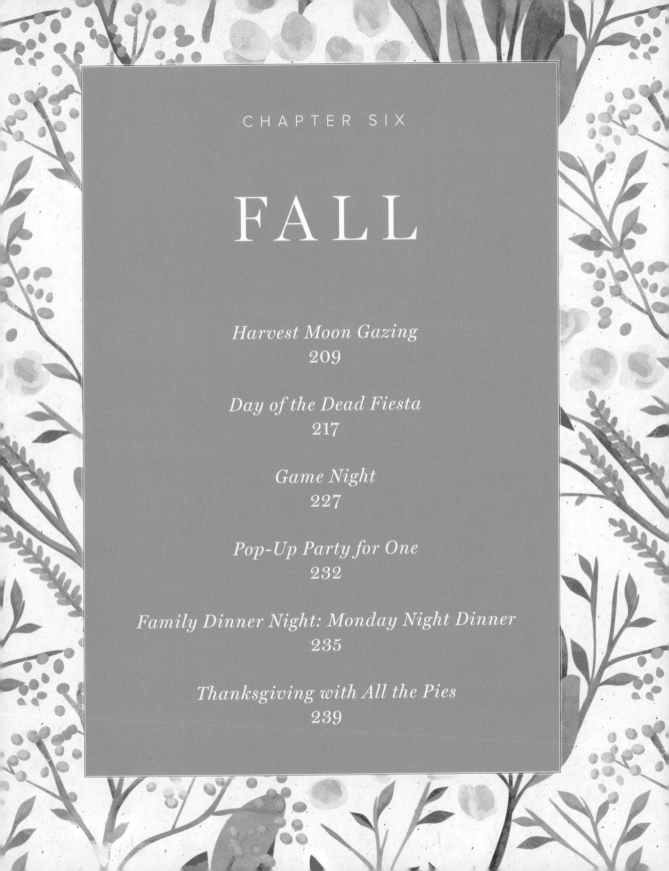

CHAPTER SIX

FALL

Harvest Moon Gazing

The harvest moon is the full moon that is nearest to the official beginning of fall and usually lands in September or October. Its bright light was said to aid the harvest, hence the name. To me, though, it's the ultimate symbol of letting go. The start of fall means letting go of summer and all the life that bloomed and blossomed while the weather was warm. And according to ancient rituals and practices from a number of cultures, including Ayurveda, the full moon can help us let go of stagnant energy, break bad habits, and release ourselves from thoughts that don't serve us. Because it takes the moon about twenty-nine days to revolve around Earth and because a woman's menstrual cycle is an average of twenty-eight days, it's believed that the moon and women are kindred spirits. When we honor the moon, we honor that we can create positive change in our lives, we honor that we can welcome new energy into our lives to replace the stale and the old, and we honor ourselves as women. That's why this is a particularly powerful time to gather your female tribe for a special night of connecting, reflecting, resolving, and letting go.

Do It Easy

HEALING COMMUNAL COOKING

Instead of preparing a full spread of nourishing foods for your guests, turn that into one of the activities of the evening. Something that I find so rewarding and special is getting in the kitchen with my friends and working together to make a meal. I also love exploring new cookbooks (like *One Part Plant* and *The Moon Juice Cookbook*) and cooking sites (like *The Chalkboard Mag*) for recipes that use tons of plants and maybe healing ingredients, such as certain herbs and spices, that I normally don't use in my day-to-day meal prep. Think of a book or website that inspires you and choose three to five recipes for the night, depending on how many people are coming over. Aim for one or two lighter dishes—a soup, salad, or spread—two main dishes, and a dessert. Stick with recipes that won't take longer than an hour to make, and consider including only recipes free of gluten, dairy, meat, and processed sugar, which are acidic in nature and can trigger disease-causing inflammation in the body. This allows the grains, vegetables, herbs, fruits, and healthy fats to do all their body-scrubbing magic. Clean, whole foods are what keep our bodies healing and our minds clear. They help flush out the things we don't want (toxins, excess weight, feelings of insecurity or anxiety) and invite in the things we do want (radiant health and a sense of calm, clarity, and contentment). That's definitely in keeping with the theme of the evening!

The day before the party, go grocery shopping for all the ingredients you'll need, wash the produce, and get started on any prep that will take longer than the time you want to be cooking (e.g., roasting vegetables or marinating any items). Think about how you want to divide up the group and assign the recipes—maybe use this event to acquaint friends of yours who have never met one another, or let the group divide itself up. Then make copies of the recipes so every person in each group can have her own.

The day of the party, get your guests excited for the meal they'll be making by setting out the ingredients in a beautiful display. Dedicate an area like your kitchen or dining room table to the bounty like an altar of deliciousness and good health. Use vases, pitchers, and jars to make bouquets of fresh herbs and greens; mound the vegetables into bowls grouped by color; put spices and dried herbs into small bowls so everyone can take in their gorgeous color and intoxicating smell. If there are ingredients that people might not have cooked with before—turmeric root, lemongrass, millet—give a little rundown of how they're used and what they taste like. Look it up online if you don't know!

Do It Right

TAKE A MOON BATH

We've all heard of sunbathing and how getting just a little kiss of sun can be beneficial for our bodies; it helps set our internal clock, stokes our emotional fires, and gives us our fix of vitamin D. Well, according to Ayurvedic healers, *moon* bathing can be just as valuable. The light of the moon is a positive, restorative energy that grounds us and lends a sense of calm and rejuvenation. It's even thought to have a cooling effect on the body, which balances "hot" or inflamed conditions like hypertension, hives or rashes, and chronic pain. Regardless of what you believe, taking the time to lie in the grass under the moon in good company is a soothing, cleansing exercise that will have you breathing a little bit more deeply.

MOON BATH 101

✴ GATHER IN A CIRCLE: If you don't have enough yoga mats or blankets for everyone, have guests bring their own. Arrange them in a circle, either on your lawn or, if you don't have the space and are feeling adventurous, at a nearby park or beach. Have everyone take a seat.

✴ GET ON THE SAME PAGE: Explain that you're all about to get comfy and gaze at the moon—or close your eyes—for fifteen minutes and describe the significance and benefits of the exercise. Suggest that everyone have a question in mind to focus on as you bathe. Things like: *What clarity am I seeking from the full moon about challenges that I'm facing? How can I harness the energy of the full moon to help me achieve my goals? What do I need to focus on until the next full moon?*

✴ BATHE! Set a timer for fifteen minutes and invite the quiet. If you have speakers that you can set up outside, play relaxing music or sounds.

✴ SHARE: Encourage people to share any thoughts or feelings that came to them during the meditation.

✴ HAVE A RELEASE CEREMONY: To fully embrace the spirit of letting go, have everyone write down anything she wants to officially let go of: fears, worries, bad habits, stagnation. With a lit candle or over a bonfire or fire pit, have everyone burn away what she no longer wants to carry with her.

✴ CLEANSE THE SPACE: Burn sage or palo santo to clear out all the negative stuff that everyone has let go of over the course of the night and to seal in all the lovely energy created there.

soma milk

In Ayurveda, "soma" is the element of ourselves ruled by the moon—the same elements that we soak up when we bathe in its light. This vedic drink is thought to enhance soma production in the body and mind and is ritually enjoyed while basking under the light of the full moon. It was traditionally made using plant extracts whose identities have never been confirmed, so now nut or coconut milk is used in its place and infused with warming, heady spices like cardamom, cinnamon, nutmeg, and vanilla.

When your evening's festivities are drawing to a close and your guests are full with the spirit and possibility you've created together, give everyone a small glass of this milk to send them off to sweet dreams.

In a small saucepan over low heat, combine all the ingredients. Stir and heat for 10 minutes. Remove the pan from the heat and let cool for 15 minutes. Pour the liquid through a fine mesh strainer into a pitcher or large jar. Serve warm.

SERVES 6

4 cups unsweetened almond, cashew, hemp, or coconut milk

2 tablespoons honey, maple, or brown rice syrup

2 vanilla beans, halved lengthwise

6 cardamom pods

2 cinnamon sticks

½ teaspoon grated nutmeg

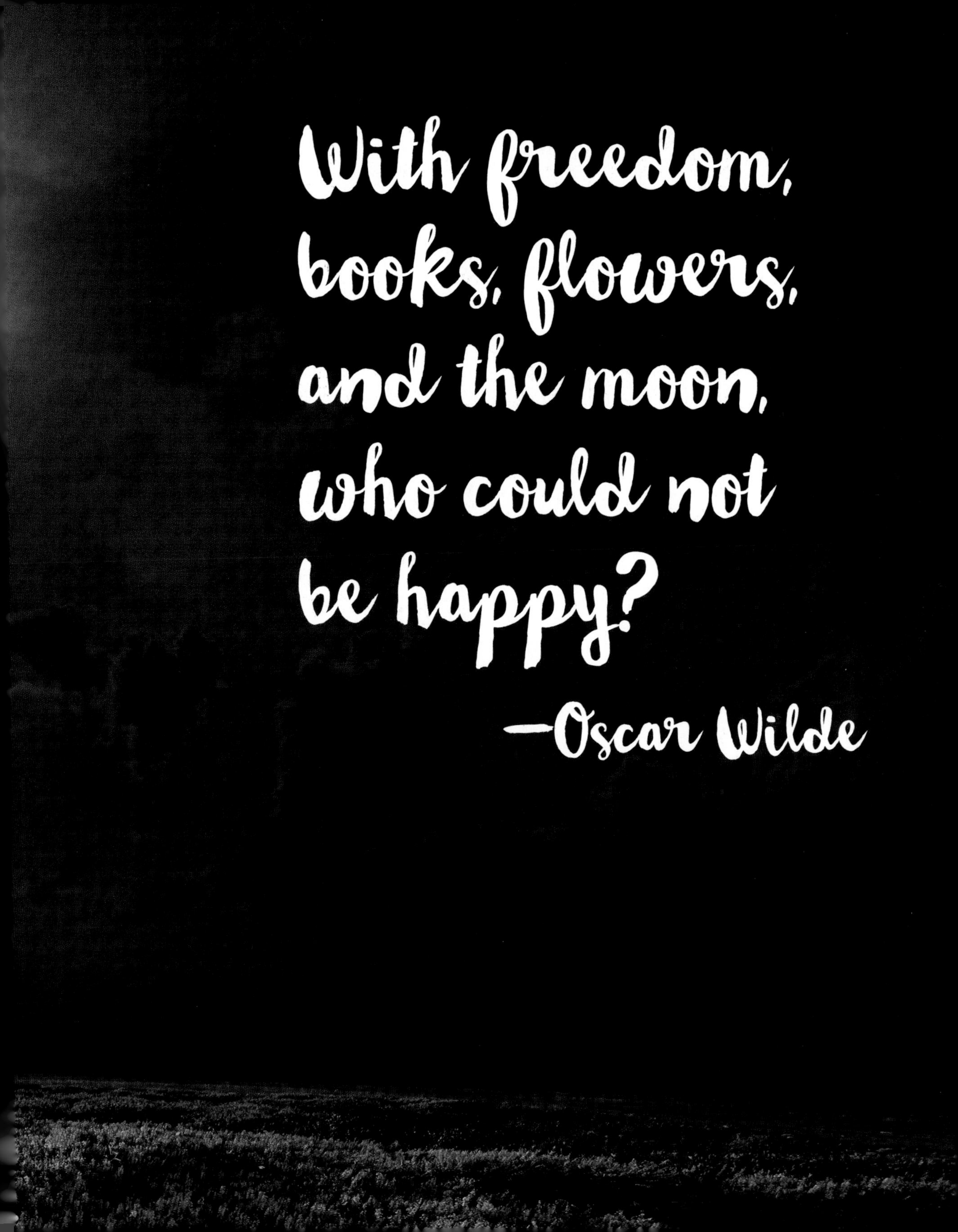

With freedom,
books, flowers,
and the moon,
who could not
be happy?

—Oscar Wilde

Day of the Dead Fiesta

Day of the Dead, or Día de los Muertos, is like Halloween's more introspective, connective cousin. It's a holiday with Mexican roots and is a time when celebrants believe that the dead will come back to visit the living on earth for just one day. For this sorrowful but joyous reunion, friends and family come together to remember those close to them who have died, visiting their graves or greeting their spirits with altars and small gifts, before sending them off once again on their long spiritual journey back to whatever world they dwell in. There are religious undertones to the experience, but at its heart is the opportunity to gather with your tribe and support one another as you honor the loved ones who are no longer with you—no matter your religion or faith. But the Day of the Dead is not about grief or sadness—it's for celebrating life!

Think festive and bright for this celebration. What better way to remember those we have loved and lost than to fill the room with beautiful colors, music, and even drinks. Bring in a cool, other-worldly element like a tarot card or palm reader to fortify your connection with the spirits and to add another layer of meaningful introspection to the evening.

Do It Right

ASSEMBLE AN ALTAR

To root your party in the true intention of Día de los Muertos, designate a small table in your space as an altar. Traditionally, those who observe this holiday build altars, or *ofrendas,* in their homes as a way to welcome the deceased after their very long, difficult journey to the land of the living, as well as to act as a beacon to guide the souls home. That's why you'll typically find bright, fragrant flowers—such as marigolds, chrysanthemums, and gladioli—incense, and lots of candles. People will also offer up photographs of their loved ones, in addition to their favorite foods and beverages, special possessions, or other small gifts. Some people build a three-tiered altar to symbolize the underworld, earth, and heaven. Some drape their altar with a colored tablecloth to symbolize a certain meaning: purple for mourning, pink for celebration, white for purity and hope, orange for the sun, red for the blood of life, and yellow as the light to lead the spirit to the altar. And some include a festive-looking array of *calaveras,* or skulls, made from either sugar or clay and decorated in bold colors. Interpret these traditions however they resonate with you.

To make the evening meaningful to your guests, ask that they bring something to contribute to the altar: a picture, a talisman that represents who their loved one was or what that person meant to them, a significant belonging, or even a favorite snack. Arrange your altar with candles for guests to light.

FOOD AND DRINK FOR THE LIVING

The Day of the Dead is meant to be a celebration of us reuniting with the souls of our loved ones who have passed and of us reuniting with our loved ones who are still living. That most certainly calls for plenty of food and drink. My favorites would be a super-sized bowl of spicy, smoky mezcal punch and a help yourself burrito bowl bar. But just because this holiday comes from Mexican traditions doesn't mean you have to stick with that vibe for food and drinks. The idea behind Día de los Muertos is that you're offering up something that you and your spirit-world visitors love.

Day of the Dead is meant to be a celebration of us reuniting with the souls of our loved ones who have passed and of us reuniting with our loved ones who are still living.

Do It Easy

BURRITO BOWL BAR

A burrito bowl bar means very little prep, a simple setup, and an easy hand-held dinner for your guests. Plus, any leftovers can be put to good use as a healthy meal option during the week. Start with a base of cooked rice (brown, white, or both), then put out lots of options for doing it up: black or pinto beans; grilled or ground chicken; steak or ground beef; shrimp; guaca-mole; an assortment of salsas: green, red, fresh, and jarred; sour cream; fresh veggies like corn, tomatoes, and onions; fajita-style veggies; and plantains (okay, I know those aren't Mexican, but their slightly sweet goodness is *so* yummy in a burrito bowl). Don't forget a decked-out selection of hot sauces.

For your tablescape, carry over some of the elements from your altar, taking care not to turn the spread into a parody of the holiday: a bold-colored tablecloth, vibrant flowers and garlands, maybe some *calaveras,* and lots and lots of candles. Use the colors from your linens and floral arrangements to coordinate your serving pieces and plates.

grapefruit-jalapeño mezcal punch

Like tequila, mezcal is made from the heart of the agave plant, but unlike tequila—where the agave is heated in large stainless-steel drums—the agave for mezcal is cooked in pits over a wood fire, which gives it a caramelized, smoky flavor. It's delicious on its own, but it also makes a sultry addition to cocktails. For Día de los Muertos, I wanted to come up with a large-batch punch so I didn't need to play bartender all night, and in the spirit of the holiday, I wanted it to be spicy and brightly colored. The result: grapefruit juice spiked with jalapeño-infused simple syrup, a generous pour of mezcal, and a splash of club soda.

If you don't have a large punch bowl to set this out in, make a spread of just the components—the juice, simple syrup, and mezcal premixed in a large pitcher or carafe; cans or bottles of club soda; a small platter of sliced grapefruit; ice—and write little signs describing how guests can DIY.

In a small pot, combine the honey and 1 cup water. Bring to a boil while stirring, until the honey is fully dissolved. Add the jalapeño and let the mixture boil. Reduce the heat and simmer for 10 minutes. Remove the pot from the heat and let the syrup cool completely. Strain the syrup and set aside.

In a large glass punch bowl, combine the grapefruit juice, mezcal, and club soda with 1 cup of the simple syrup. Taste and adjust the flavor to your liking, adding more syrup, mezcal, or juice if necessary. Garnish with grapefruit slices. Serve the punch over ice.

SERVES 10

1 cup honey

3 jalapeños, halved lengthwise

4 cups grapefruit juice

2 cups mezcal

2 cups club soda, chilled

1 grapefruit, sliced thin, for garnish

Ice

gluten-free baked mini-churros with dairy-free dulce de leche

These mini-churros are about as healthy as you can possibly get with a dessert that's usually fried—and still totally delicious (and adorably festive). Complete with a dulce de leche dipping sauce that's unbelievably rich, yet free of dairy and processed sugar.

Preheat the oven to 400°F. Cover 2 baking sheets with parchment paper or silicone baking pads and set aside.

In a medium bowl, whisk the eggs with 1 tablespoon of the cinnamon and the vanilla. Set aside.

In a medium saucepan, stir together the brown rice syrup and salt with 1 cup water. Add the butter and raise the temperature to medium-high heat. Heat until the butter is melted and the mixture starts to boil. Remove the pan from the heat and add the flour, and flaxseeds, stirring with a wooden spoon to break up any clumps. The mixture will start to take on a doughy consistency and pull away from the sides of the pan. Stir in the egg mixture until fully incorporated.

Transfer the dough to a piping bag fitted with a 1-inch star tip or a large Ziploc bag with the corner snipped with a 1-inch opening.

Pipe the dough into 3-inch pieces on the prepared baking pans. Leave about 2 inches between the churros.

Bake for 10 to 12 minutes, rotating halfway through, until the churros are cooked through and golden brown. Re-

MAKES ABOUT 20 MINI-CHURROS

2 large eggs

1 tablespoon plus 1 teaspoon ground cinnamon

1 teaspoon vanilla extract

2 tablespoons brown rice syrup

½ teaspoon salt

⅓ cup unsalted butter

2½ cups Bob's Red Mill Paleo baking flour

¼ cup ground flaxseeds

¼ cup granulated sugar

move from the oven and let cool slightly before transferring to a wire cooling rack.

On a plate or in a shallow bowl, combine the granulated sugar and remaining 1 teaspoon of cinnamon. Roll the churros in the cinnamon-sugar coating and serve immediately.

DAIRY-FREE DULCE DE LECHE

Combine all the ingredients in a blender and blend until smooth. Adjust the consistency with water as desired. Store at room temperature for 2 to 3 days or in the fridge for 2 to 3 weeks. The mixture will solidify when it gets cold, so leave it at room temperature for a couple of hours before serving or gently warm it in a pan.

MAKES ABOUT 1½ CUPS

1 cup packed pitted medjool dates, soaked in warm water for 15 minutes

¼ cup plus 1 tablespoon warm water

¼ cup brown rice syrup

1 teaspoon vanilla extract

½ teaspoon fleur de sel

Game Night

Game night is a pretty big deal in my house. In fact, I'm *all* about it, and I'm not talking about a few people sitting around playing Trivial Pursuit. To me, it's not game night unless basically all your friends and their friends (and sometimes *their* friends) show up ready to get down to business. Seriously, don't come to game night at my house if you're not going to do game night! We all get really pumped up and *really* competitive. (Beware: People's true colors come out at game night. Be prepared to see the jerkiest winners and sorest losers!) But no matter what, it always ends up being a super-fun time—and such a heart opener. As I've said before, there's nothing like play to feed the spirit and help you connect to a more carefree wavelength.

Instead of breaking up a crowd into individual game stations, I like for everyone to play together, so we all get a chance to hang out. We usually go with the game Mafia, or a version called Werewolf, which can include as many people as you want (look up the rules online), but if we hit the forty-person mark (trust me, it has happened!), we push all the furniture out of the way and play a crazy game of running Charades. We break into teams and move to different parts of the room with our groups. The rules are a bit complicated, so I suggest you look them up online. But the fun comes in the "running" part, which is literally running toward the moderator in the center of the room. Trust me, it's a blast. During the night, every so often we take breathers for a drink refresh and a bite to eat, and decide if we want to go for another round.

The great thing about game night—especially if you stick with interactive games that don't rely on special boards or gear—is that there's very little setup. A great spread of food, which we'll get into, is really all you need besides your crew and a good attitude, and even that I like to keep very low fuss.

Pretty Fun Party Tip: This is one of those parties where you need to be able to read a room. If people look like they're having a great time just hanging out after one game feeling the music and just soaking up one another's company, then maybe you should let things ride and enjoy the night. Ask around and get a feel for whether people want to play another game. If they do, take the lead: turn off the music and make the announcement that it's time to play another round. (Did I mention I'm serious about game night?) If you get more than a few noes, well, game night is over and it's time to party.

Do It Easy

For me, the guest list for game night is anywhere from fifteen to forty-five people—it's a big one. And it's all about one thing and one thing only: playing games. So keep the drinks plentiful and the food simple. I love finger foods for game night, so I don't have to manage a ton of plates and silverware (paper and plastic, obviously). One of my go-tos is a batch of easy (and veggie-stuffed) baked meatballs, plus a traditional antipasti spread of Italian classics: breadsticks, cured meats and cheeses, dried or fresh fruit, olives, roasted peppers, shrimp cocktail, the works.

The goal of this particular antipasti spread is to keep it *easy*. You can do your shopping days in advance, since everything will keep well in the fridge, and definitely don't feel like you need to be a hero and make your own mozzarella or even steam your own shrimp. Have your fish guy or gal do it for you! (And defer to them on how much you need to buy for your crowd.) Then put together a collection of tasty-sounding items from the grocery store or specialty food store, sticking with an Italian theme to keep the offerings feeling cohesive. Then pick one spot in your house as the designated food and drink station, ideally somewhere out of the way of your game—the kitchen is great for this. Either on your kitchen table or counter, arrange a wood board or two with any meats or cheeses you've collected, slicing a few pieces off of each to encourage people to dig in. Scatter the boards with dried or fresh fruit—pick two or three kinds, tops—then add little bowls of things like olives, sun-dried tomatoes, and roasted red peppers and a platter for your meatballs and one for your shrimp and cocktail sauce, if you're going that route. Finish it off with a bouquet of breadsticks in a tall glass or jar, or add another board for slicing up a loaf of bread. As one last touch, look in your local crafts store or party goods store—or online—for festive toothpicks so guests can grab, dip, and nibble without getting their hands dirty.

Game night is all about one thing and one thing only: playing games.

baked mini-meatballs

These Italian meatballs taste just as rich as Nonna's, but are baked instead of pan-fried and use lean meat with a small hit of bacon—so they're not nearly as heavy or greasy as the original. Plus, they're stuffed with tons of mushrooms, giving them an earthy flavor along with all their fiber-rich, immune-boosting benefits.

**MAKES ABOUT
30 MINI-MEATBALLS**

1 pound lean ground beef

2 slices bacon (about
   2 ounces), finely chopped

1 cup mushrooms, finely
   chopped

1 medium carrot, grated
   (about ½ cup)

1 small yellow onion, grated
   or finely chopped, with
   excess liquid squeezed
   out (½ to ¾ cup)

3 garlic cloves, minced

1 large egg

¼ cup finely chopped fresh
   parsley

3 tablespoons grated
   Parmesan cheese

1 tablespoon bread crumbs

1 teaspoon salt

½ teaspoon freshly ground
   black pepper

Preheat the oven to 400°F.

Place all the ingredients in a large bowl and mix until just combined. Pinch off enough of the mixture to create a 1½-inch meatball and cook it in a pan with a little oil until browned on each side, about 3 minutes total. Taste and adjust the seasoning for the batch, if necessary. Roll the rest of the mixture into 1½-inch meatballs and arrange them on a wire rack set on a large rimmed baking sheet. Bake until cooked through, about 15 minutes.

Do It Right

If you're looking for somewhere to splurge on a game night, see if there are any local food trucks—especially taco trucks—that you can hire to set up shop for a few hours outside your house. It's a total crowd pleaser and lets you off the hook food wise, 100 percent.

GAME ON!

I love game night for so many reasons, aside from it being good, easy fun. Play is good for the soul, and is almost primal in the way it makes us feel. It elevates all the happy chemicals in our brain, and competition (the good kind) is also a positive thing because it can make us sharper and quicker—and it always leads to laughter. Make game night part of your celebration practice. Trust me, you won't regret it.

Pop-Up Party
for One

Consider this your reminder to put as much intention into creating a space for yourself as you would for a group of people. Also consider this your reminder that every once in a while, it's important to take the time to do absolutely nothing. It's not an indulgence; it's self-care. That said, this isn't when you meditate and think about life; it's when you just relax and think about nothing except being really nice to yourself. Even if it's just an hour and a half, shut off your phone, pull on your loosest, comfiest sweats and fuzzy socks, and set your own cozy stage. Think about a scene in a television show or film of someone in their house, relaxing. What does that look like? Now create that for yourself: light candles, put on music, make a nest out of blankets and pillows. Maybe put together a nice tray with all your favorite things. For myself, that would include my current knitting project (to work on while I watch some brainless television), ordered-in sushi, my favorite frozen yogurt, and a cup of tea. And then I tell anyone in the house who isn't already asleep, "This is Mommy's party, and you're not invited." (I'm kinda kidding, not really!!)

Even though you're not spending this time to meditate or be actively mindful, that doesn't mean that positive things aren't happening. Spending quality time alone can be majorly beneficial. According to researchers at Harvard University, these retreats from the rest of the world can rev up our creative juices, helping us have more innovative ideas—perhaps because we're removed from the judgment of others. It also helps us strengthen our sense of empathy, because the clearer we are about our own emotions, the more in tune we can be with others.[10] It's also thought to help us form even stronger bonds with the emotions of others[11] and relieve symptoms of depression.[12] Consider this your ammo the next time you talk yourself out of that much-needed break!

Even though you're not spending this time to meditate or be actively mindful, that doesn't mean that positive things aren't happening.

Family Dinner Night: Monday Night Dinner

Monday nights can be tough—you're coming out of a weekend, which usually means you're exhausted from running around with the kids, and you're staring down the entire week ahead of you. That's usually enough reason to literally phone it in, calling in takeout and letting everyone drift in and out of the kitchen in their own blue Monday stupor. But Mondays are so important in a family's rhythm—it's how you set the tone for the rest of the week. Even with all the chaos of what you need to get done now that you're back to normal life after the weekend, try to take a minute for everyone to check in, let one another know that you have each other's backs no matter what's on the docket over the next five days, and maybe even set an intention, especially if there are big or stressful things going on: a test, a meeting, a doctor's appointment, a tryout or an audition. It's like your team's huddle before the big game!

roasted chicken with root vegetables

I used to think the key to amazing roasted chicken was doing all kinds of *stuff* to it: buttering under the skin, packing it with herbs and aromatics, brining it, pre-salting it, sending it to the spa for a week . . . Well the secret to super-moist, super-golden, super-crisp-in-all-the-right-places chicken is just—wait for it—seasoning with salt and pepper. And then rotating the bird in the pan every 20 minutes for an hour. That's it.

Meet your new go-to weeknight dinner. It takes almost no time to prep—it's essentially all oven time—and is possibly the most comforting meal that exists. You can switch up the veggies depending on the season, and use any leftover meat for things like potpies, tacos, or salads throughout the week.

Take the chicken out of the fridge 1 hour before cooking.

Preheat the oven to 400°F.

Cut the sweet potato and the root vegetable into 1-inch pieces. Scatter them on the bottom of a cast-iron skillet or roasting pan, and toss with just enough olive oil to coat and a generous pinch of salt.

Pat the chicken dry with a paper towel. Season with salt and pepper and set the bird breast side up on top of the veggies. Roast for 20 minutes, then turn the chicken breast side down. Roast for another 20 minutes. Turn the bird breast side up once more and roast for a final 20 minutes. It should be golden brown and fully cooked, with an internal temperature of 165°F, and the veggies should be caramelized and tender. Let the chicken rest for 10 to 15 minutes before carving.

SERVES 4 TO 6

One 3½- to 4-pound chicken
1 medium sweet potato
1 medium turnip, rutabaga,
    large parsnip, or other
    root vegetable
Olive oil
Kosher salt, to taste
Black pepper, to taste

Thanksgiving with All the Pies

Thanksgiving is one holiday where family traditions hold strong, so far be it from me to tell you to change it up! There's obviously no right or wrong way to celebrate this wonderful day so long as it feels genuine to you. The best part about Thanksgiving is that it has intention infused right into the holiday: Give thanks and eat! So long as you can do it surrounded by people whom you love and who love you, there's not much more you need to do to make the day meaningful. But it's also fun to take this mega-holiday and really go for it with food, décor, and of course, gratitude.

Even though our menu is almost always the same—yam-stuffed oranges! Grandma's broccoli surprise! pies for days!—the décor is a *very* different story. I like to turn the fancy factor way up when it comes to setting the table. Since it's one of the few times a year I'll host a super-sophisticated sit-down dinner, I love the excuse to pull out all the over-the-top stops, which is basically a master class in all the elements we've talked about throughout this book. I establish a chic theme, build a formal table concept from the linens to the chargers to the dishes and glasses, use just about every piece of silverware I own (and in some cases pieces I don't, but more on that in a bit), make sure the lighting in the room feels cozy and intimate, and use everything in my tablescape toolbox, such as flowers, candles, and elements from nature, to make the room feel elevated but welcoming and warm. The rest of the evening is hardly what you could call formal; you can't get our family together—all twenty-plus of us, not including any strays we invite—without someone or everyone breaking into song and dance or something else ridiculous and silly. There will be wine spilled on the table, pie smashed into the rug, and generally a big glorious mess—but at least we started out with a gorgeous spread!

Thanksgiving do's and don'ts:

* **Do** go back to the **Drawing Board**. Ask yourself what colors you want to showcase, what you want your theme to be. Feeling super-traditional? Go for golds, oranges, and browns. Want to change it up? Do what I did one year and channel an enchanted English garden. Get creative with your inspiration, which could even be a pretty leaf that you found on a walk. Then use those decisions to inform everything else. This is one party where you shouldn't be shy about going all out. Just keep coming back to the vibe you want as a touchstone so things don't start feeling scattered.

* **Do** use any heirloom or hand-me-down linens, dishes, silverware, or serving pieces to summon the spirit of those who can't be with you on this special day.

* **Do** decide where you're going to put all the food. Setting up buffet-style means more room for tablescape flourishes, versus accommodating a serious spread. And definitely give the desserts their own festive moment on a sideboard or table, adding interest by varying height with things like cake pedestals and platters or plates set on top of overturned (and matching) bowls.

* **Do** think of all the pretty touches, such as cloth napkins, napkin rings (one of my favorite ways to add a little extra *sumthin'* to a table), carafes for water and any other beverages, salt and pepper cellars, and sweet bowls and dishes for condiments, especially butter bells (I *love* a butter bell!).

* **Do** keep table decorations low so you can see everyone's face.

* **Do** set an extra place or two at the table, just in case. If your house is like mine, you never know who's going to show up.

* **Don't** be afraid to get super-swish with your place settings, with bread dishes and butter knives; three sets of forks and spoons (the more silverware, the more seriously swanky a table looks); chargers, dinner plates, and salad plates; and seating assignments (it can take care of that awkward moment when everyone's wondering where to sit).

* **Don't** feel like you need to do everything yourself, even if you're like me and will probably try to anyway. Make life a *little* easier—and so much more enjoyable—by asking a few trusty sidekicks to come early to help prep. I'm sure I'm not alone in thinking that some of the most fun and special moments happen when everyone's together in the kitchen. And *definitely* let people bring things if they ask!

* **Don't** think that formal = no fun. Make getting dinner on the table a group effort. Give everyone a job—including the kids—from rolling out dough to lighting the candles, then crank up the Ella Fitzgerald or Frank Sinatra and keep the wine flowing. Major bonus points if there's singing or dancing by the time you sit down.

* **Don't** forget what it's all about. Ask everyone to share what they're thankful for. Even though everyone's been daydreaming about the mashed potatoes, and the turkey has made the house smell amazing, *this*

————

is what today is for. Hit the pause button on all the tumult, invite everyone to settle in, and say a few words of gratitude of your own: Thank people for coming, give a special mention to anyone who contributed to the meal or the evening in some way, and share what makes today so meaningful to you. Your sincerity will help set the tone for everyone else. Then hold the space while your guests take turns sharing thanks of their own. After that, *time to eat*!

Do It Easy

WHEN IT PAYS TO RENT

Bringing in things like plates, glassware, and silverware is lower maintenance than you'd think. Most rental companies offer a range of options when it comes to price, and it means you 1) don't need to buy extra place settings to accommodate a crowd; 2) won't need to spend a ton of time cleaning up after dinner (since most companies just ask that everything be rinsed); and 3) can change it up from year to year when it comes to style.

THANKSGIVING EVE PIE PARTY

When it comes to Thanksgiving, pies are my *thing*. Every year I make about nine of them. Yep, you read that right! There's just something about pie that I love so much: graham cracker crust pies; flaky, buttery crust pies; cream-filled pies; fruit-filled pies; mini-pies; lattice-top pies; old-school standbys; and tricked-out newcomers. And I've definitely tried them all: banana cream pie (my number one go-to), key lime pie (a new addition and a huge hit), single-serving pumpkin pies (I mean, how adorable?), and the Thanksgiving pie to end all pies, Caramel-Apple-Pecan Pie (yes, the recipe follows). My pies don't look like from-the-bakery pies either. I like getting out my cookie cutters and decorating with leaves, hearts, and other pretty touches. To make sure I don't totally lose my mind, I make all the components for the pies in stages over the course of about three days, so by the night before Thanksgiving all I need to do is assemble and bake. And because a lot of my friends have to be with their families on Thanksgiving Day, pie-making is the perfect excuse for us to have our own Thanksgiving gathering to celebrate how much we appreciate one another. There's not much more to it than a lot of good music, a lot of spilled flour, and a lot of laughter. And in the spirit of pie, I love whipping up a couple *pizza* pies for everyone to graze on while I put them to work.

When it comes to Thanksgiving, pies are my thing. I like getting out my cookie cutters and decorating with leaves, hearts, and other pretty touches.

greatest-hits-pie

This pie has a little bit of everything and a little something for everyone—crust with a rich, sweet layer of caramel, classic apple pie filling, a pecan crumble, and more caramel drizzled over the top. It really is the queen of Thanksgiving pies, and the perfect project for putting your friends to work the night before the big day. While I'm not the kind of girl to buy pie dough, don't be shy about taking the shortcut! If you do decide to go for it, I highly recommend you invest in a container of Nutiva coconut shortening. It's free of the hydrogenated fat that you usually find in traditional vegetable shortenings, plus it's organic, non-GMO, and Fair Trade Certified.

MAKE THE CRUST: Combine the flours, sugar, and salt in a food processor. Pulse a few times to mix. Sprinkle the butter into the bowl and pulse another 5 or 6 times to mix. Use a fork to break up the mixture, lifting the heavier parts of the mixture from the bottom of the bowl. Sprinkle the shortening into the bowl and pulse 5 or 6 times. Gently toss the mixture again with the fork. Pour half of the water over the flour mixture and pulse another 5 or 6 times. Toss again. Add the remaining water and pulse until the dough starts to look like coarse crumbs.

Transfer the mixture to a large bowl. Squeeze a bit of the dough between your fingers—if it crumbles instead of packs together, sprinkle a teaspoon of cold water over the dough and work it in with your fingers. Form a ball with the dough. On a lightly floured surface, knead the ball a couple of times, and then shape it into a ¾-inch-thick disk. Wrap the dough in plastic and refrigerate for 1 hour or overnight.

SERVES 8 TO 10

For the crust

1 cup all-purpose flour
½ cup whole wheat flour
3 tablespoons sugar
½ teaspoon salt
¼ cup (½ stick) cold unsalted
    butter, cut into ¼-inch
    pieces
¼ cup cold vegetable
    shortening (I like Nutiva),
    cut into pieces
¼ cup cold water
10 store-bought caramels,
    roughly chopped

greatest-hits-pie (continued)

On a sheet of lightly floured parchment paper, roll the dough into a 13-inch circle with a floured rolling pin. Carefully flip the dough over a 9½-inch deep-dish pie pan, making sure the dough is centered, and then remove the parchment paper. Use your fingertips to tuck the dough into the pan, without stretching it, and press the dough up the sides to create a roughly ½-inch ridge above the rim of the pan. Scatter the caramel pieces over the dough in the bottom of the pan and place it all in the freezer while you make the filling.

Preheat the oven to 400°F.

MAKE THE FILLING: In a large mixing bowl, combine the apples, brown sugar, and lemon juice. Mix well and set aside for 5 to 10 minutes to macerate. In a small bowl, combine the granulated sugar and cornstarch. Stir the mixture into the fruit along with the cinnamon, nutmeg, and vanilla. Pour the filling into the chilled pie shell and use a rubber spatula to smooth the top. Put the pie on the center oven rack and bake for 30 minutes.

MAKE THE PECAN CRUMBLE: In a food processor, combine the flour, pecan halves, granulated sugar, and salt. Pulse to coarsely chop the nuts. Add the butter and pulse until the mixture resembles breadcrumbs. Transfer the mixture to a medium mixing bowl, then rub it between your fingers to form slightly larger crumbs. Refrigerate until ready to use.

Remove the pie from the oven and reduce the temperature to 375°F. Carefully and evenly spread the pecan crumble over the top of the pie. Use your fingers to pat it down lightly. Set the pie on a baking sheet and return it

For the filling

2⅓ pounds Granny Smith apples (about 7 apples), peeled, cored, and sliced

½ cup firmly packed light brown sugar

1 tablespoon fresh lemon juice

2 tablespoons granulated sugar

1 tablespoon cornstarch

½ teaspoon ground cinnamon

½ teaspoon ground nutmeg

1 teaspoon vanilla extract

For the pecan crumble

¾ cup all-purpose flour

¾ cup pecan halves

½ cup granulated sugar

¼ teaspoon salt

6 tablespoons (¾ stick) cold unsalted butter, cut into ¼-inch pieces

For the caramel drizzle

3 tablespoons unsalted butter, cut into pieces

30 store-bought caramels

For serving

½ cup pecan halves
½ cup chopped pecans

to the oven, rotating it 180 degrees from how it was originally placed in the oven. Bake until the filling is bubbling around the edges, 30 to 40 minutes. If the top starts to get too dark, cover the pie with loosely tented aluminum foil. Transfer the pie to a wire rack and let cool for about 1 hour.

MAKE THE CARAMEL DRIZZLE: While the pie is still warm, combine the butter, caramels, and 1 tablespoon water in a large heatproof bowl set over a small pot of barely simmering water. Melt the caramels, pressing down with a rubber spatula to help them soften. Once the caramels are completely melted, whisk the mixture until it's smooth. Drizzle the caramel over the pie, immediately arrange the pecan halves on top (get creative with a design!), and sprinkle with the chopped pecans. Let cool for 1 hour before serving.

easy-as-pie spicy kale–ricotta pizza

When it comes to my Thanksgiving pies, there's no other way than from scratch. But for pizza to eat while making these confections? I say give yourself a break and do it semi-homemade, especially because you can buy premade dough from most grocery stores and just about any pie shop. You could also put these toppings on a sprouted or gluten-free crust, or even on tortillas (just reduce the cooking temp to 425°F and time to about 5 minutes).

And to make your life even easier, this version doesn't require a pizza peel or stone, just a large rimmed sheet pan or cast-iron pan. This style of pizza is simple, and the dough gets a little extra luscious and crispy from cooking in olive oil. But it's not all over-the-top decadence for this pie; since this time of year usually means overdoing it on *everything,* I've loaded up this pizza with lots of good-for-you-from-head-to-toe kale, plus a touch of ricotta and mozzarella cheese and a hit of crushed red pepper for spice. Add a salad, and dinner is served.

In a large bowl, toss the kale with 2 tablespoons olive oil and the lemon juice to coat. Season with a generous pinch of salt and pepper. Massage or squeeze the kale with your hands until the leaves start to soften, about 2 minutes. Set aside while the dough comes to room temperature.

Remove the pizza dough from the fridge and let it sit at room temperature for about 1 hour, which will help it be more pliable (aka stretchy) when it comes time to put it in the pan.

Preheat the oven to 550°F, or as high as it will go.

Drizzle the remaining 2 tablespoons olive oil in the bottom of a large rimmed baking sheet pan. Use your hands

SERVES 6

1 bunch Tuscan kale, ribs and stems removed, torn into 1- to 2-inch pieces
¼ cup extra virgin olive oil, plus more for serving
2 tablespoons fresh lemon juice
Kosher salt
Freshly ground black pepper

1 ball store-bought pizza
   dough
1 cup fresh ricotta
8 ounces fresh mozzarella,
   torn into quarter-sized
   pieces
Crushed red pepper flakes,
   to taste
¼ cup grated Parmesan
   cheese

to coat the entire bottom. Carefully stretch the dough so that it covers just about the entire baking sheet. Be careful not to rip any holes in it!

In a small bowl, season the ricotta with salt and pepper to taste. Spread the ricotta over the dough, leaving about a ½-inch border around the dough for the crust. Top with the kale, making sure to leave any excess juice in the bowl and not on the pizza, and dot with the mozzarella. Bake for 8 to 12 minutes, until the crust is golden brown and the cheese is bubbling and golden. Sprinkle with the red pepper flakes and Parmesan, and drizzle with a touch more olive oil. Transfer the pizza to a cutting board and let it sit for just a minute or two— restraint!—then slice and serve.

CONCLUSION

CHECKING IN

AS I SAID earlier in this book, a celebration practice is about *doing*. Just as you can hone your skills only if you actually use them, you can get better at throwing parties or gatherings only if you actually do it. And now that you've read about all the amazing mind-body-spirit benefits of getting people together—plus all the delicious recipes and fun themes—I'm hoping you realize how important a part of self-care this all can be, and make it a priority to sprinkle a little more celebration and tradition into your life.

Another great way to continue building these skills and your confidence is to do a little emotional inventory after the last bit of confetti has been vacuumed up. Sure, you can reflect on things like *Was there enough food?* or *Could I have made things simpler for myself?*—and keep track of the answers so you can improve on these things the next time—but more important, see how you're feeling. Ask yourself:

Did it allow you to express your creativity?

Did it allow you to create new traditions with friends and family?

Did it allow you to really enjoy the best parts of life—not food and drink, but the love we feel from others?

I sincerely hope that the lessons I've had the pleasure of learning will find their way into your celebration practice and, what's more, infuse your life with as much happiness and meaning as it has mine. If we all continue to gather with a little more heart, a little more love, and a little more intention, we have the power to make the world a much more special place. And for that, I thank you! Last but certainly not least, I wouldn't be a gracious hostess if I didn't send a heartfelt thank-you to you for joining me on this journey.

Do you feel

pretty happy?

Pretty connected?

Pretty grateful?

Then you probably had

PRETTY FUN!

ACKNOWLEDGMENTS

Writing a book is kind of like throwing a party—it wouldn't be the same without the wonderful people who contribute to the process and the fun. I'd like to thank the people who helped me shape this book.

I would like to thank Carrie Thornton, my editor extraordinaire; cheers to another book built on passion and vision and fun.

Thank you to Cait Hoyt at CAA, my stellar agent; Madeleine Ali, my second hand, brain, and heart; Rachel Holtzman, my brilliant writing partner; and Amy Neunsinger, my amazing photographer.

I would also like to thank the entire Dey Street Books team, including Sean Newcott, Lynn Grady, Ben Steinberg, Heidi Richter, Shelby Meizlik, Kelly Rudolph, Jeanne Reina, Mumtaz Mustafa, Owen Corrigan, Nyamekye Waliyaya, Andrea Molitor, Serena Wang, Suet Chong, and Lucy Albanese.

Most importantly, I'd like to thank my Mom, Pa, and beautiful children for all their love and support, as well as my extraordinarily fun family and friends with whom I can't wait to celebrate at the next party!

NOTES

1. http://www.apa.org/monitor/2010/04/dance.aspx

2. http://www.huffingtonpost.com/pascal-vrticka/human-social-development_b_3921942.html

3. "The Health Benefits of Strong Relationships," *Harvard Women's Health Watch*, December 2010, http://www.health.harvard.edu/newsletter_article/the-health-benefits-of-strong-relationships.

4. Umberson, D., & Montez, J.K. (2010). Social Relationships and Health: A Flashpoint for Health Policy. *Journal of Health and Social Behavior, 51* (Suppl), S54-S66. http://doil.org/1001177/0022146510383501.

5. Robert A. Emmons and Michael E. McCullough, "Counting Blessings Versus Burdens: An Experimental Investigation of Gratitude and Subjective Well-Being in Daily Life," *Journal of Personality and Social Psychology* 84, no. 2 (2003): 377–89. Available at http://greatergood.berkeley.edu/pdfs/GratitudePDFs/6Emmons-BlessingsBurdens.pdf.

6. "Health Benefits of Strong Relationships."

7. Ibid.

8. https://thefamilydinnerproject.org/about-us/benefits-of-family-dinners/

9. Jonathan S. Kaplan, "Plants Make You Feel Better," *Psychology Today,* March 11, 2009, https://www.psychologytoday.com/blog/urban-mindfulness/200903/plants-make-you-feel-better.

10. Leon Neyfakh, "The Power of Lonely," *Boston Globe,* March 6, 2011, http://archive.boston.com/bostonglobe/ideas/articles/2011/03/06/the_power_of_lonely/?page=full.

11. Ester Buchholz, "The Call of Solitude," *Psychology Today,* January 1, 1998, https://www.psychologytoday.com/articles/199801/the-call-solitude.

12. Reed W. Larson, "The Emergence of Solitude as a Constructive Domain of Experience in Early Adolescence," *Child Development* 68, no. 1 (February 1997): 80–93. Available at http://www.jstor.org/stable/1131927?seq=1#page_scan_tab_contents.